40
46
48

The

DEGROWTH AND SUSTAINABILITY

p54   Self-interest is a
powerful aid to wilful
blindness

'Publishers have created lists of short books that
discuss the questions that your average [electoral]
candidate will only ever touch if armed with a
slogan and a soundbite. Together [such books]
hint at a resurgence of the grand educational
tradition... Closest to the hot headline issues are *The
No-Nonsense Guides*. These target those topics that
a large army of voters care about, but that politicos
evade. Arguments, figures and documents combine
to prove that good journalism is far too important
to be left to (most) journalists.'

Boyd Tonkin,
The Independent,
London

About the author
Wayne Ellwood is the author of the best-selling *No-Nonsense Guide to Globalization*, which is currently in its third edition. He established the North American office of New Internationalist and worked as a co-editor of the magazine until 2010. He has also worked as an associate producer with the groundbreaking BBC television series *Global Report* and edited the reference book *The A-Z of World Development*. He has travelled widely in Asia, Africa and Latin America. He lives in Toronto, Canada, where he is an editorial consultant and writer.

Acknowledgements
Thanks to Peter A Victor for kindly agreeing to write the foreword and for his important contributions to the degrowth and sustainability debate. Thanks also to Herman Daly for his pioneering and influential work in ecological economics; to Britain's New Economics Foundation for bringing growth issues to public attention; and to David Suzuki for his passion, vision and dedication to the environment.

About the New Internationalist
New Internationalist is an independent, not-for-profit publishing co-operative that reports on issues of global justice. We publish informative current affairs and popular reference titles, complemented by multicultural recipe books, photography and fiction from the Global South, as well as calendars, diaries and cards – all with a global justice world view.

If you like this *No-Nonsense Guide* you will also enjoy the *New Internationalist* magazine. The magazine is packed full of high-quality writing and in-depth analysis, including:
- The Big Story: understanding the key global issues
- The Facts: accessible infographics
- Agenda: cutting-edge reports
- Country profile: essential insights and star ratings
- Argument: heated debate between experts
- Mixed Media: the best of global culture.

To find out more about the **New Internationalist**, visit our website at **newint.org**

The **NO-NONSENSE GUIDE** to

DEGROWTH AND SUSTAINABILITY

Wayne Ellwood

New Internationalist

The No-Nonsense Guide to Degrowth and Sustainability
First published in the UK in 2014 by
New Internationalist™ Publications Ltd
Oxford OX4 1BW, UK
newint.org

Series editor: Chris Brazier
Design by New Internationalist Publications Ltd.
Cover image: Corbis Images

Printed by T J Press International, Cornwall, UK, who hold environmental
accreditation ISO 14001.

MIX
Paper from
responsible sources
FSC® C013056

British Library Cataloguing-in-Publication Data.
A catalogue record for this book is available from the British Library.

Library of Congress Cataloging-in-Publication Data.
A catalog for this book is available from the Library of Congress.

ISBN 978-1-78026-123-2

Foreword

In the earliest days of the Industrial Revolution, the classical economists feared that any improvement in living standards above subsistence would be temporary. Economic growth would be a passing phase, succeeded by reversion to a steady-state economy where most people would be poor. Writing in the mid-19th century, John Stuart Mill was the first economist to write positively about the end of economic growth. His commentary on the costs of economic growth expressed well the concerns that occupy a growing number of commentators today. Pressure on the natural world, anomie and alienation, confusion of material gains with real prosperity, the general hustle and bustle of modern life – all were observed by Mill 150 years ago.

Despite the considerable influence on economics of his *Principles of Political Economy* (1848), Mill's critique of economic growth was largely ignored, and not just by economists. In the late 1950s this began to change, starting when several quite prominent authors took up where Mill had left off. They offered penetrating analyses of modern economies where all was clearly not well. A number of these contributions, and many which came after, inform the arguments so cogently presented by Wayne Ellwood in *The No-Nonsense Guide to Degrowth and Sustainability*.

In this short and readable book, Ellwood describes the many ways in which economies are dependent on the environment for energy and material resources, for disposal of all kinds of wastes into the air, water, on and under the land, and for a variety of 'ecosystem services' such as pollination and flood control, without which human economies could not function. He explains that economic growth has placed an unsustainable burden on the planet's resources and life-support systems to meet increasing demands from today's massively expanded population and economies.

Foreword

Ellwood rejects the argument that the answers to our problems, particularly in the rich countries, lie in yet more economic growth. He points out that all too often, the highly touted gains in efficiency from new technologies are overwhelmed by the increasing scale of economies that grow without limit and make a bad situation worse, not better.

It is rare, but not unknown, for original thinkers to be effective communicators of their ideas to the general public. In today's world, where institutional divisions distinguish 'academics' from people who make their living communicating ideas to the public, those who develop new ideas rely heavily on others to disseminate them. Typically, professors write for their academic peers and their students, leaving it to authors with a flair for communication to disseminate their ideas more broadly. The advent of social media has changed this a little, but it remains generally true that without the determined efforts of writers like Wayne Ellwood, important ideas such as degrowth and sustainability would likely remain on the periphery of public discussion and debate. In light of the seriousness of the economic, environmental and social issues that we face, this would be a serious loss, depriving the public and our governments of frameworks of thought and principles of action needed to guide us through these difficult and challenging times.

Of course, sustainability is not really a new idea. It has been the mantra of farmers and foresters for a very long time. That it should be applied to considerations of the economy is, however, more recent, dating back to the 1980s. Degrowth is even newer, only about 15 years old. Wayne Ellwood explains what these ideas mean and why we should pay attention to them. If you are curious about them, as I hope you are, then do read on.

Peter A Victor PhD, Professor in Environmental Studies, York University, Toronto, Canada

CONTENTS

Introduction

The warning signals flash briefly across our TV and computer screens; scattered headlines appear in our newspapers and magazines. The messages are disparate but unambiguous: 'Natural disasters forced 32 million from their homes in 2012'; 'Pollution threatens world's poor'; 'Why the world's weather will be going to extremes'; 'Inequality undermines democracy'; 'Burnt-out planet or financial doom?'; 'Record urban growth poses challenge'.

The facts on the ground tell a disturbing story, if we choose to listen. But life gets in the way – school, family, work, the daily battle to survive – so few of us make the time to connect the dots.

Until recently that included me. A few years ago I researched and edited a special issue of *New Internationalist* magazine on economic growth. I'd read widely on sustainability and dipped into the burgeoning field of ecological economics so it was a natural segue. Plus I've been a keen student of economics most of my adult life, wading through the business pages, gamely trying to keep up with the twists and turns of the global economy, tracking how the rich and powerful manipulate the system to their advantage. I'm an amateur, but even highly trained, professional economists rarely step outside the dominant paradigm. Combing through the critical literature on growth I began to pay attention to the big picture. It wasn't long before the scattered bits of information began to gel into a coherent whole.

A clear line emerged, connecting the dominant growth model to world-shaking social and environmental issues: widespread habitat destruction, the loss of biodiversity, chaotic shifts in global weather, the steady depletion of natural resources, growing income inequality, the debt-laden and crisis-prone global economy. The more I read, the more I discovered all these things circled back to growth.

Then I began to think: maybe growth is not the solution to our problems, maybe it *is* the problem. And the reason we can't see that is because we're thoroughly immersed in a worldview that says the *only* way to prosperity and well-being is by growing and expanding the economy.

Forever.

But as the pioneering economist and systems analyst, Kenneth Boulding, once said: 'Anyone who believes exponential growth can go on forever in a finite world is either a madman or an economist.' Nearly 50 years ago, Boulding saw the writing on the wall. In his 1966 essay, *The Economics of the Coming Spaceship Earth*, he described the 'closed' economy of the future 'in which the earth has become a single spaceship, without unlimited reservoirs of anything, either for extraction or for pollution, and in which, therefore, man must find his place in a cyclical ecological system'.

A failure of imagination

Humankind as one part of a cyclical ecological system: that notion now seems both logical and obvious. We know intuitively that nature and culture are co-dependent. We are beginning to understand that we cannot destroy the planet without destroying ourselves. Yet the gap between understanding and action is hard to bridge. Inertia is a powerful barrier to change. The growth system continues to define the contours of our world. This is as much a failure of imagination as of policy.

A few years after Kenneth Boulding, another radical critique of economic orthodoxy surfaced in the best-selling *Limits to Growth*, a ground-breaking study that had the moxie to suggest that growth carried within it the seeds of its own destruction.

The idea that human enterprise was bounded by bio-physical limits was a wake-up call that provided fuel for an embryonic environmental movement. But it was soon forgotten in the giddy surge of deregulated markets that exploded in the 1980s. Barriers to the free flow of capital were eliminated; financial speculators ruled in a computerized world, holding entire countries to ransom. The ethos of unlimited consumerism easily migrated across borders in the digital era. Giant factory trawlers vacuumed the seas. Vast monocultures of genetically modified crops fed by petrochemicals replaced native grasslands and forests. Deep-pocketed mining companies expanded their restless search for resources from the Arctic to the Amazon. It was, in other words, growth as usual.

The argument that the resources of the Earth have a limit is self-evident. More to the point, as the environmental footprint analysis shows us, we are already past those limits, consuming irreplaceable natural capital at a rate that is jeopardizing the well-being of future generations. We have put growth ahead of sustainability to the extent that sustainability has become a marketing tool, an excuse for more of the same. We can no longer grow the economy and strive for sustainability. The two concepts are mutually exclusive.

Economic meltdown

The failure of the dominant growth model has been painfully evident since the global economy collapsed in 2008. Triggered by footloose investors, a weak regulatory structure, delusional bankers and an enormous US real-estate bubble, the whole creaking edifice teetered on the brink of disaster. The global credit web, the circulatory system of world capitalism, slipped into paralysis as major banks hunkered down and refused to lend to each other.

With the ghost of the Great Depression of the 1930s hovering in the background, politicians eventually saw the light and closed ranks. In Europe, North America, Australasia – even in China – governments injected massive liquidity into floundering markets, bailing out distressed banks and major corporations in a united-we-stand effort to save global capitalism from its own excesses. Millions of workers lost their jobs as companies cut costs.

In total nearly $16 trillion in public funds (mostly interest-free loans) were used to prop up the international financial system. The intervention helped to stave off immediate financial disaster in the shape of a severe global depression. Credit gradually started to move again, trade slowly resumed, corporations and banks once again became profitable. But it was a grudging kind of recovery.

Unemployment remains unacceptably high in most Western nations, with grievous social fallout. Poverty is increasing as the gap between rich and poor widens. Food banks are doing a booming business. Governments face massive budget deficits, mainly because of the billions in debt they took on to underwrite the economic recovery. Meanwhile, the corporate sector points to public debt as the source of our economic troubles. The irony is that the debt was first contracted to bail out those same banks and corporations. Instead the cry is for 'balanced budgets' to restore 'market confidence'.

This is the medicine we supposedly must take to nurse the economy back to health: cuts in government services, sale of public assets, reduced pensions, redundancies, stagnant wages and tax breaks for the wealthy. Nearly half a decade after the crash, we're back where we started. We wait for growth to save us while ordinary people take the hit.

The assumption has always been that growth will make things better. In fact you could say that growth is the escape valve for modern capitalism. Without it, the poor would have good reason to grumble. With it, tomorrow will always be brighter. If we just keep ramping up the GDP, things will improve. Michael Mandelbaum of the Johns Hopkins School of Advanced International Studies summed up this view when he said that 'economic growth is necessary to keep the promise... that each generation will have the opportunity to become more prosperous than the preceding one, the popular term for which is the American Dream.'

The measuring stick for growth is Gross Domestic Product (GDP), which is basically a laundry list of all the things we produce, usually divided by population to give us GDP per capita. As a measurement of human progress, this is a very rough-and-ready metric. How can it not be when it mixes up 'bads' and 'goods'? Anything that has a dollar sign attached to it contributes to GDP. Oil spills, suburban sprawl, war and crime are lumped together with steel production, medical consulting fees and the value of this year's wheat crop.

But the indication now is that the price we pay for growth exceeds the benefits. The balance has tilted to the increasingly worrying downside – what the writer Herman Daly calls 'uneconomic growth'.

Only this time there's a difference. There's a growing recognition that the global economic system is rigged in favor of the wealthy, the top 1% who run the show.

In September 2011, a few thousand folks pitched tents in a corporate-owned park in the heart of lower Manhattan. 'We are the 99%,' was their slogan. The 'Occupy Wall Street' (OWS) movement was a mix of jobless college graduates, single moms, social activists, union members, clergy, concerned citizens and others. The message was clear, even if the alternatives weren't. The protest was against the corporate takeover of the international economy, against economic inequality, against the continuing destruction of the environment and called for social justice and a different vision for the world.

The OWS movement was initially overlooked by the corporate media, but it soon spread via the internet and social media until it could no longer be ignored. Other 'Occupy' movements popped up in dozens of cities around the globe – from Toronto, Montreal and San Francisco to Sydney, London and Paris – in an effort to spread the message of dissatisfaction with the global economy. Growth was not specifically the target of the protests. But it was certainly the subtext.

The 'Occupy Wall Street' movement is the most recent sign of a more extensive global phenomenon. There has been a wave of social and political turmoil and instability since the world lurched into economic chaos. The 'Arab Spring' caught the attention of the world, igniting political change across North Africa and the Middle East while causing dictators elsewhere to be on alert. There were riots in London. In Spain, Italy and Greece, citizens faced with painful austerity measures staged mass public demonstrations. Chilean students took to the streets to bring attention to economic inequality and rising tuition fees while Israel experienced its largest demonstrations in decades when hundreds of thousands of middle-class citizens protested high housing prices and falling living standards. Even in the two economic powerhouses of the developing world there were signs of dissatisfaction. There is growing impatience and disgust with corruption in India and mounting unhappiness with inequality and environmental damage in China.

Finding a better path
There has to be a better way and that's what this book is all about. Sustainability and degrowth are, in many ways, very old ideas rooted in traditional spiritual and humanist notions of husbandry, stewardship and community. But they are also two very loaded terms.

In this *No-Nonsense Guide* I've attempted to unpick those concepts and to think about what it means to live in a world where growth reigns supreme. With each passing day it's increasingly evident that the prevailing model is leading us down a dangerous and ever-narrowing path. We need what used to be called a 'paradigm shift'.

A decade ago, a global opposition movement provoked by the ravages of economic globalization declared that 'another world is possible'. If anything, that alternative vision is even more urgent today as we face a future of life after growth. We need to redefine what we mean by prosperity but, more critically, we need to ask fundamental questions about the end goals of our frenzied economic activity. What is an economy for? Do we want an ever-growing GDP and 'sustainable growth'? Or do we want to reshape our economic project to sustain people, communities and the natural world? With a sense of common purpose we can avoid environmental collapse and pave the way for a more convivial future. Without this great transformation, we risk lurching from crisis to crisis, compromising the fate of the generations who will follow us.

As Kenneth Boulding warned: 'There is a great deal of historical evidence to suggest that a society which loses its identity with posterity, and which loses its positive image of the future, loses also its capacity to deal with present problems, and soon falls apart.'

Wayne Ellwood
Toronto, 2013

1 The growth machine

The unquestioning devotion to the idea of constant economic growth is a fairly recent phenomenon in human history. But it has taken firm hold despite the numerous great thinkers who have pointed out what should be clear to all – that in a world of finite resources, exponential growth is not only unsustainable but also extremely dangerous.

'The difficulty lies, not in the new ideas, but in escaping from the old ones, which ramify, for those brought up as most of us have been, into every corner of our minds.'

John Maynard Keynes

The eminent British biologist Charles Darwin was a careful scientist – meticulous, patient and rigorous. He spent five years at sea on a research ship, *The Beagle*, collecting data, then nearly 20 years sifting his research, honing his analysis and polishing his prose, before publishing *On the Origin of Species*, his groundbreaking work, in November 1859.[1]

Darwin's slim volume was what we would call a 'game changer'; a revolutionary work that irrevocably and fundamentally altered the way human beings see themselves and the natural world. Today, most of us are familiar in a general way with his theory of 'natural selection' – the foundation of modern evolutionary biology. But 150 years ago, things weren't so clear-cut. Darwin was sailing into choppy waters. The Church of England set rigid boundaries on scientific thought and his thesis was clearly offside – a challenge to the orthodox Biblical view that humans were a separate, unique part of God's creation and that all life was divinely concocted and unchangeable. The establishment mocked him. There was intense public debate. But Darwin stood his ground and eventually, with the support of Thomas Huxley (aka 'Darwin's bulldog') and others, his radical insights found acceptance.

Darwin's core idea that all animals and plants evolve and adapt through natural selection is now the bedrock of modern life sciences. He unlocked the door to a new way of understanding the history of life on Earth – although 'junk science' theorists, religious fundamentalists and 'intelligent design' proponents are still trying to slam it shut.

History of an idea

For most of human history, economic growth was a mere blip. Societies developed slowly, economies were founded on subsistence and growth was minimal. Only the last eight generations of humans have experienced consistent growth (out of an estimated 125,000 generations in total). 'Historically, steady state is the normal condition; growth is an aberration.'[2]

The modern idea of growth is a product of the 17th- and 18th-century European Enlightenment that challenged traditional views of religion and humankind's place in the cosmos. Thinkers like John Locke in England, David Hume in Scotland, Voltaire in France and Thomas Paine in the US mapped out this new intellectual terrain.

This rupture with tradition changed age-old *cyclical* thinking to *sequential* thinking, unleashed democratic political movements and ushered in the rule of law. The idea of progress became paramount: the notion that history has a direction, which is the gradual improvement of the human condition. The rise of science and the empirical method merged with improved technologies (the steam engine, gunpowder, the printing press), stimulating early capitalism. Economic growth became synonymous with social progress, development and human improvement. European colonialism then spread the 'growth equals progress' idea around the world.

But it wasn't until the Second World War that our modern understanding of growth began to enter the consciousness of governments and international agencies. According to one scholar, 'there is hardly a trace of interest in economic growth as a policy objective in the official or professional literature of Western countries before 1950'. Pumping up the war machine proved that growth could be rapid, if necessary, and pointed the way to future expansion. In 1943 the US National Resources Planning Board reported to President Roosevelt: 'Our expanding economy is likely to surpass the wildest estimates of a few years back and is capable of bringing to all of our people freedom, security and adventure in richer measure than

Darwin's long battle has disturbing echoes today. Like his detractors in Victorian England, we are also mired in an illusion that blocks our understanding of critical forces at work in the world. But the myth that envelops us – our blind faith in limitless economic growth – is more dangerous and even more deeply rooted.

We have abiding faith that the economy will grow forever, that there are no limits to the wealth we can create from the natural resources of this bountiful planet. Our financial systems are premised on growth;

ever before in history.'³ Less than two decades later, the future US President Ronald Reagan summed up this view during his stint as host of a hugely popular 1950s TV drama programme sponsored by General Electric. Every Sunday night a young, rock-jawed Reagan confidently told American viewers: 'Progress is our most important product.'

In his 1978 book, *The Rise and Fall of Economic Growth*, HW Arndt adds that a statement by the US Council of Economic Advisors in October 1949 'was perhaps the first explicit official pronouncement in favour of economic growth as a policy objective in any Western country'. With the arrival of the 'Cold War' in the 1950s and growing tensions between the Soviet Union and the West the notion of growth took on another dimension. Increasing per-capita GDP was trumpeted as a measure of who was winning the battle between two contending economic systems. Within a few decades, growth became the ultimate metric of progress and economic health around the world. As Arndt notes, the case for economic growth was based on the belief that steady, rapid and indefinitely increasing productive capacity was the key to higher living standards, which were both 'desirable and demanded' by the citizenry of the world.

This slavish devotion to growth economics still dominates the mindset of governments, mainstream economists and their uncritical boosters in the media, trade unions, big business and academia. All major power groups in society now assume that a growing economy is the *sine qua non* of social progress. As long as a rising tide lifts all boats, it's full steam ahead and we can avoid hard choices.

As the former World Bank Chief Economist and ex-president of Harvard University, Lawrence Summers, put it: 'We cannot and will not accept a "speed limit" on American economic growth. It is the task of economic policy to grow the economy as rapidly, sustainably and inclusively as possible.'⁴ ■

Adapted from Peter A Victor, *Managing without growth*, Edward Elgar, 2008.

government policies are based on growth; corporate profits, jobs and incomes are hitched to growth.

Growth equals prosperity. The equation has been drummed into us for so long that it has become received wisdom. Growth brings employment, wealth, material and social progress, happiness and stability. Growth is the key to combating poverty. It makes the world a better place.

Indeed, an unwavering belief in progress is the quintessential modern idea. History is linear. Science, technology, democratic governance and liberal humanism greased by native ingenuity, will lead to the improvement of the human species. And economic growth is the vehicle for arriving at that destination.

Loosening bolts in the growth engine

But lately the bolts have begun to loosen in the growth engine. The global environment is under severe stress and has already been irreparably damaged. In 2005 the UN Millennium Ecosystem Assessment, a collaborative work of more than 10,000 scientists, found 60 per cent of 'ecosystem services' – things like climate regulation, the water cycle, pollination, global fisheries, natural waste treatment – were degraded or being used unsustainably.

'Human activity is putting such a heavy strain on the natural functions of the Earth,' the report warned, 'that the ability of the planet's ecosystems to sustain human endeavor can no longer be taken for granted.'

But discounting the environment is only part of the problem – and one that we will explore in depth in a later chapter. There are also a growing number of thinkers who are beginning to challenge the status quo in fundamental ways by asking hard questions.

What if the emperor has no clothes? What if endless economic growth is a chimera that causes more problems that it solves?

Many ecologists believe we have entered an era of

'uneconomic growth' where more fevered economic activity actually depresses living standards and levels of happiness. It doesn't take much of a stretch to see what they mean. We can have a booming economy alongside growing inequality and fewer jobs – i.e. jobless growth. We can have shopping malls full of digital gadgets and showrooms replete with bigger, shinier automobiles – but how much better off are we if we spend three hours a day in traffic jams, worry over bigger debts and have less time for ourselves and our families? The volume and pace of growth tell us nothing about the quality of growth. And shouldn't that be our main concern?

But before we get too caught up in the downside of growth, let's backtrack for a moment to answer some basic questions. What exactly do we mean by economic growth? How does it work and why has it become so central to our lives?

Today, the standard measure of growth is Gross Domestic Product or GDP – the total value of all goods and services produced in a country within a given period. It's usually calculated over the course of a year. GDP as a measure of growth is now so entwined in our lives that it's barely given a second thought. It's one of those things that most people don't question: more is good; less is bad. You only need to peruse the avalanche of daily media reports to validate this assumption. Here's an edited snippet from a recent news report that gives you an idea of how commonplace the language of growth/GDP has become.

Global outlook turns darker
...Calling the risks of a worldwide slump "alarmingly high" as it warned of decelerating economies, the IMF puts the odds of global growth falling below 2 per cent – effectively a recession – at one-in-six.

At that rate of growth, the global economy is too weak to keep up with population growth.

'A key issue is whether the global economy is just hitting another bout of turbulence in what was always expected to be a slow and bumpy recovery or whether the current slowdown has a more lasting component,' the IMF said in its 'World Economic Outlook', released in advance of the annual World Bank-IMF meeting in Tokyo...

The IMF sliced its global growth forecast to 3.3 per cent this year from 3.5 per cent in its previous reading in July, which would mark the slowest expansion since 2009, when the world was emerging from the deepest slump since the Great Depression.

The influential agency has also reduced its projected growth in 2013 to 3.6 per cent from 3.9 per cent just three months ago and 4.1 per cent in April. But it warned ominously that even the lower projection for 2012 and beyond 'depends on whether European and US policy-makers deal pro-actively with their major short-term economic challenges.'[5]

This typical press report underscores a key concern: without GDP growth the global economy faces collapse. We're hostage to the way our economy is structured. And we know what that means. We've seen ample evidence of the human pain and suffering that faltering growth can bring since the economic downturn of 2008. Mass unemployment, a shrinking tax base, slashed public services, shuttered factories and shops, increasing homelessness and hunger.

In the Eurozone, hard-pressed countries like Greece and Spain have been hammered by European Union austerity measures. The rationale is that short-term pain will bring long-term gain. In 2010 nearly a million Spaniards depended on the Catholic

Relentless rise

The total value of goods and services produced worldwide doubled from 1991 to 2011 – to nearly $78 trillion. In the decade before the 2008 slump the global economy grew by an average 4% annually. Western industrial economies typically grew about 3% in the decade before the recession. But by 2011 that had fallen to just 1.6%. Growth in developing economies suffered less during the recent recession. They grew 6% annually in the decade before the 2008 recession and 6.2% in 2011.

Gross World Product, 1950-2011

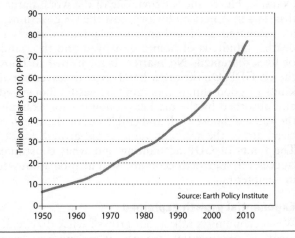

Source: Earth Policy Institute

charity Caritas for food and the number has jumped since then. In that same year more than 22 per cent of Spanish households were living in poverty and nearly 600,000 of them had no income at all. With youth unemployment over 50 per cent, scavenging has become so common that the town of Girona has installed locks on supermarket garbage bins as a public health precaution.[6] The situation is no better in Greece, where the recent financial crisis has caused around a quarter of the country's workers to lose their jobs, driving thousands of protesters into the streets.

Yet by any standard GDP is a faulty measure of prosperity. It distinguishes neither between the costs and benefits of growth nor between its quality and quantity. You might say it measures what can be counted rather than what counts, confusing 'goods' with 'bads'. Any economic activity that has a price tag attached is rolled into the calculation of GDP. The cost of car accidents, pollution abatement, heart operations, cancer care, making weapons: they're all included. For example, Hurricane Katrina, one of the worst natural disasters in American history, cost the US government an estimated $114 billion and resulted in scores of deaths, hundreds of homes destroyed and thousands of lives disrupted. No matter. It all helped to boost the US GDP. On the other hand, growth leaves out all kinds of good things that can't be easily 'monetized' and absorbed by the market economy – for example, the value of housework and childcare, or the worth of clean air, or the aesthetic value of old-growth forests. The limits of GDP accounting and what constitutes 'success' in a growth economy will also be addressed in Chapter 6.

Exponential growth explained

When economists talk about growth what they really mean is *exponential* growth. If a number grows yearly by a certain fixed amount it will double in size after so many years. It all depends on the percentage growth rate: the higher the rate, the faster the doubling time. Statisticians use a rough method of measuring doubling times called the 'rule of 70'. Divide the rate of growth into 70 and you'll come up with the time needed for the initial quantity to double. If an economy is growing at 5 per cent a year, for example, it will take 14 years for it to double. An economy growing at 10 per cent will take 7 years to double. You see what exponential growth can do.

Let's take China's recent phenomenal growth to

illustrate what this means in the real world. Over the past decade China's economy has been growing by double digits. Recent turmoil in the global economy has knocked back GDP growth to just under eight per cent. Still, the country's economy is doubling approximately every ten years. What does this mean in terms of resource consumption and pollution? Lester Brown of the Earth Policy Institute has crunched the numbers. China already consumes more grain, meat, coal and steel than the US – though on a per-capita basis China's consumption is, of course, a lot less. However,

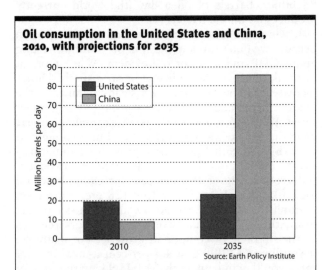

Oil consumption in the United States and China, 2010, with projections for 2035

Source: Earth Policy Institute

According to the Earth Policy Institute: 'What China is teaching us is that the Western economic model – the fossil-fuel-based, automobile-centered, throwaway economy – will not work for the world. If it does not work for China, it will not work for India, which by 2035 is projected to have an even larger population than China. Nor will it work for the other three billion people in developing countries who are also dreaming the "American dream". And, in an increasingly integrated global economy where we all depend on the same grain, oil, and steel, the Western economic model will no longer work for the industrial countries either.'[7] ■

Brown estimates that at current growth rates Chinese per-capita income will equal the US 2011 level by 2035. And when that happens? Assuming the Chinese will spend their income like Americans, Brown says that China would then consume 80 per cent as much paper as is produced globally today and 70 per cent of the yearly grain harvest. He also estimates the country would have 1.1 billion automobiles (the world now has just over a billion) and would need to pave two-thirds of its rice-growing land for roads and parking lots. To power this leap in consumption would require 85 billion barrels of oil a day (the world currently produces 86 billion barrels).

It's important to understand exponential growth because we don't think about it in our normal fretting about GDP and it is not self-evident. When most of us think of growth we think of linear growth. Things increase incrementally but by a steady number so the amount being added is always constant. The number series 1,2,3,4,5,6 and so on is an example of linear growth. So is 2,4,6,8,10,12 etc. But exponential growth (also called geometric growth or sometimes compounding growth) is very different. An exponential growth rate of 100 per cent for example would look like this: 1,2,4,8,16,32,64,128 etc. Plotted on a graph the action starts slowly, and then skyrockets dramatically. It's what investment advisors refer to as the 'miracle of compound growth'. For example, if you invest $1,000 at a 4.5-per-cent annual interest rate, you'll wind up with $1,045.94 at the end of one year. The second year's interest is then 4.5 per cent of $1,045.94 and so on. At the end of 30 years you'd have a total of $3,847.70. But exponential growth really begins to explode as time increases. If somehow you discovered the fountain of youth and lived to 150, your initial $1,000 would have ballooned to $736,959.41!

The UK-based New Economics Foundation (NEF)

uses the analogy of a hamster whose weight doubles weekly to illustrate the concept of compound growth.

'From birth to puberty a hamster doubles its weight each week. If, then, instead of leveling-off in maturity as animals do, the hamster continued to double its weight each week, on its first birthday we would be facing a 9-billion-tonne hamster. If it kept eating at the same ratio of food to body weight, by then its daily intake would be greater than the total annual amount of maize produced worldwide. There is a reason that in nature things do not grow indefinitely.'[8]

In nature, of course, growth is inevitably constrained by physical limits and a complex interplay of natural relationships. If the food supply for one species increases, then the population of that species will multiply to take advantage of the available food. Soon more predators will be attracted to the expanding numbers and the growing population will eventually deplete the food source and numbers will plummet. Nature is a hard taskmaster. A boom is always tempered by a bust.

Malthus and Mill

Herein lies our dilemma. Our current economic model is based on the notion of endless growth. Yet we live in a bounded, finite world, a world with physical limits. In the end the two are irreconcilable. How can increases of population, industrial production and limitless consumption continue, forever, on a finite planet?

The Reverend Thomas Malthus was one of the first thinkers to address this question in *An Essay on the Principle of Population*, first published around 1800. Malthus, an Anglican cleric, pondered the question of exponential population growth in relation to available resources and food supply. Malthus feared that global population would increase faster than the earth could support and that this inevitable trajectory would lead to widespread famine and disease.

'Must it not then be acknowledged by an attentive

examiner of the histories of mankind,' Malthus wrote, 'that in every age and in every State in which man has existed, or does now exist, that the increase of population is necessarily limited by the means of subsistence... and the actual population kept equal to the means of subsistence, by misery and vice.'

Malthus's gloomy vision was out of step with the upbeat enlightenment values of 18th- and 19th-century Europe. And, as it turned out, he misjudged the impact of science and technology on food production. The introduction of mechanized farming, combined with the spread of oil-based fertilizers and pesticides, increased harvests beyond imagination. Malthus also failed to take into account the link between falling birth rates and improved living standards. As industrialized societies became wealthier and women gained some measure of economic independence, birth rates leveled off dramatically.

Around 2,000 years ago, with the Roman Empire and the Han dynasty in China at their peaks, there were 300 million humans spread around the globe. By the time Malthus was penning his population thesis 1,800 years later there were thought to be around a billion people on the planet. By 1950, a century and a half later, that number had increased to 2.5 billion. Then the exponential growth factor really began to kick in: by 2005, just 55 years later, there were 6.5 billion people, an increase of 160 per cent. The UN now says we're on target to reach 9 billion by 2050.

But it's by no means a sure thing. A lot depends on the variable that Malthus missed, what demographers call the 'fertility rate' or the number of children a woman will have during her lifetime. Already the fertility rate is below replacement level in more than 75 countries, which means that populations are falling in those nations before migration is taken into account. Why? Well, the answer is not straightforward but it appears there is a clear link between a falling fertility rate and women's empowerment. The more economic power and the more education that women have, the more likely they are to choose to have fewer children. The UN projects future population numbers using low, medium and high fertility forecasts. With a low fertility rate (entirely feasible given current trends) the agency predicts a leveling off and then decline in world population. Numbers will peak in 2050 at 8 billion, then start to gradually decline so that by 2100 we will be back to where we were in 1998 with around 6 billion people.

But Malthus wasn't the only growth skeptic. The classical economist and philosopher John Stuart Mill reckoned that a growing economy was necessary up to a point but that eventually a 'stationary state' would be needed to replace the 'trampling, crushing, elbowing and treading on each other's heels' that characterized the rough-and-tumble nastiness of Dickensian Britain.

Mill was an economist but his interests ranged widely over philosophy and political economy. He was concerned with big issues and fundamental questions:

'Towards what ultimate point is society tending by its industrial progress? When the progress ceases, in what condition are we to expect that it will leave mankind... It must always have been seen, more or less distinctly, by political economists, that the increase of wealth is not boundless: that at the end of what they term the progressive state lies the stationary state, that all progress in wealth is but a postponement of this, and that each step in advance is an approach to it.'[9]

Mill envisaged a post-capitalist world of co-operative enterprise where greed and avarice would fade and growth would be unnecessary. Once the problems of production were solved he imagined 'a well-paid and affluent body of laborers... not only exempt from coarser toils, but with sufficient leisure, both physical and mental, from mechanical details, to cultivate freely the graces of life...'[10]

Mill was perhaps ahead of his time in predicting that endless economic growth was inevitably self-defeating. But others were to follow in his footsteps.

Soddy and Keynes

One of the most notable, but largely unsung, critics of the orthodox growth model was the British chemist-cum-economist Frederick Soddy. In the wake of World War One, Soddy was devastated by the role his fellow scientists had played in the senseless carnage. He decided to devote himself to political economy and brought his formidable scientific background to the task. (He had already won the 1921 Nobel Prize in chemistry for his work on radioactive decay.) Soddy began by looking at the laws of thermodynamics, which you may remember from your high-school physics classes.

The first law says that energy can neither be created nor destroyed; it can only be transformed from one form to another. For example, when gasoline is burned in your car's engine you are converting the original solar energy captured millions of years ago into mechanical energy, plus heat and waste exhaust. The first law leads elegantly into the second law, sometimes known as the 'entropy' law. The second law says that every time energy is converted from one form to another we lose some of the initial energy in the form of dissipated heat. What that means is that all energy use flows from low entropy to high entropy. In other words, the world is in a long downhill slide. And the higher the entropy, the less likely we are able to use that form of energy in any useful way.

What Frederick Soddy did was to apply his knowledge of physics to the money economy. In his 1926 book, *Wealth, Virtual Wealth and Debt: The Solution of the Economic Paradox*, Soddy argued that money and debt were at the root of our economic problems because they were not subject to the entropy law. Real wealth, he said, is concrete: furniture, houses, computers, farm animals, footballs, etc. This wealth, he said, is mutable and subject to decay over time. In other words real wealth is also trapped in the downward spiral of entropy. But money and debt are 'virtual wealth', Soddy wrote, abstractions subject only to the laws of mathematics. Debt, in particular, he cautioned, was a claim on future wealth, which could grow out of all proportion to the rate at which real wealth is created. Rather than decay, debt is a human construct that can grow indefinitely at any rate we decide. It is this debt as virtual wealth, according to Soddy, that is the driving wheel of growth:

'Debts are subject to the laws of mathematics rather than physics. Unlike wealth, which is subject to the laws of thermodynamics, debts do not rot with old age and are not consumed in the process of living. On the contrary, they grow at so much per cent per annum, by the well-known mathematical laws of simple and compound interest... It is this underlying confusion between wealth and debt which has made such a tragedy of the scientific era.'[11]

Soddy's thoughts on entropy and the bio-physical limits to growth were ignored at the time. But one of his contemporaries, John Maynard Keynes, was much more influential. Like Mill, Keynes was an iconoclast, a brilliant economist with a restless intellect. In the midst of the Great Depression of the 1930s Keynes advocated that government take an active, inter-ventionist role in both fiscal and monetary policy. Firm government regulation and an active fiscal policy could, he said, kick-start growth in times of economic malaise. He believed the impact of state spending would catalyze the economy, create jobs and stimulate consumption. And he was right. Keynesian economic policies slowly helped to lift the world out of depression and became the dominant tools used by Western governments to manage national economies until the era of Ronald Reagan and Margaret Thatcher in the late 1970s and early 1980s.

But Keynes was not an unthinking cheerleader of growth. He wrote at length about the ethical problems of capitalism and the 'love of money' which, he reckoned, was the driving force behind economic expansion for its own sake. An economy that places money at the center will have no cut-off point, he believed, because 'abstract money will always seem more attractive than concrete goods'. According to his biographer Robert Skidelsky, Keynes suggested that there should be 'moral limits' to growth long before the 'limits to growth' concept was first popularized in the 1970s. Those limits, Keynes wrote, should be based on a proper understanding of 'the ends of life and of the role of economic motives and economic growth in relation to those ends'.

According to Skidelsky: 'Keynes never ceased to question the purposes of economic activity... his conclusion was that the pursuit of money... was justified only to the extent that it led to the "good life". And a good life was not what made people better off: it was what made them "good". To make the world ethically better was the only justifiable purpose of economic striving.'[12]

Georgescu-Roegen and *The Limits to Growth*

Like Frederick Soddy, the Romanian-American economist Nicholas Georgescu-Roegen was also a pioneering critic of economic growth. In his 1971 book, *The Entropy Law and the Economic Process*, Georgescu-Roegen refined Soddy's analysis, arguing that the human economy is a thermodynamic system, which is ultimately dependent on the physical world and therefore constrained by what he termed 'bio-economic' limits. Entropy, he said, increases inexorably and eventually runs head on into the finite material basis of growth. Low-entropy energy and materials are combined to turn natural resources into goods, services and the inevitable waste products. It is therefore impossible to escape the limits of the physical world and the inexorable decline in the capacity of energy to do work. This perpetual winding down thus defines the limits of the human economy. Georgescu-Roegen developed his own fourth law of thermodynamics which says, in part: 'in a closed system, the material entropy must ultimately reach a maximum' which implies that 'complete recycling is impossible'.[13] He spoke of natural resources in terms of 'renewable and non-renewable stocks' and 'flows'.

These terms are now widely used in the burgeoning field of ecological economics. As the key modern theorist of entropy, Georgescu-Roegen's analysis was a major influence on this increasingly important field of study. His thought also shaped the enormously influential Club of Rome report, *The Limits to Growth*, published in 1972. In fact, Georgescu-Roegen was a close friend and confidant of Dennis Meadows, the young Harvard systems-management expert who spearheaded the groundbreaking study.

The Limits to Growth was a runaway bestseller that forcefully put the question of growth and the environment on the public agenda. It sold 12 million copies and had such wide-ranging influence that US President Jimmy Carter even commissioned a report from the Council on Environmental Quality to look at how limits to growth might impact the US economy. The report found that 'if present trends continue, the world in 2000 will be more crowded, more polluted, less stable ecologically and more vulnerable to disruption than the world we live in now. Serious stresses involving population, resources and environment are clearly visible ahead.'[14]

The Limits to Growth was a watershed because it raised fundamental questions about endless growth on a finite planet. Meadows and his colleagues used Massachusetts Institute of Technology computers to examine economic growth since the industrial revolution – this was 1972 and the use of computers to make this kind of scientific projection was in itself revolutionary. They primed the machines with data on resource use, food production, land use, population, industrial production, pollution and a host of other variables, including non-linear feedback loops between the various data sets. They then crunched the numbers and came out with extrapolations of what might happen in the next century. Their conclusions were stark and a little scary in the booming 1970s. With capitalism triumphant and the system humming along, decision-makers didn't really want to bother thinking about such things. The report concluded that, if current growth trends continued, the global economy would hit the wall sometime in the 21st century. The gradual depletion of natural resources and the fouling of the environment would combine to increase prices, collapse living standards, level populations and stop growth in its tracks. Meadows and company did not say this was inevitable, just likely without major changes to the dominant system of industrial production. Nonetheless, they came in for a barrage of criticism from both Left and Right.

From the Left the concern was that the Club of Rome that commissioned the Report was an élitist cabal of technocrats out to sabotage the poor by shutting off the growth tap. Instead of consumption, resource use and environmental limits, they focused on population and inequality, dismissing the 'limits' arguments as both premature and irrelevant to the pressing problem of poverty and social justice. The Right also dismissed *The Limits to Growth* as specious scare-mongering in a time of obvious abundance in western Europe and North America. Few mainstream economists lauded the work; most saw it as technically flawed, falling back on standard neoclassical economics to underscore their criticisms. They were especially exercised because the data failed to take into account the role of new technology and the 'price mechanism' – the notion that higher prices, by stimulating new supplies and encouraging substitution, can side-step resource depletion and open the way to perpetual growth.

Neither side really grasped the point: that we are on a collision course with the natural limits of the planet, living off our capital rather than our interest. The day of reckoning will come. We can do something about it, or we can ignore it. The choice is up to us.

In 2004, the authors published *Limits to Growth: the 30-Year Update*, which used essentially the same model as the original but updated the data. The results echoed the findings of 1972.

As physicist and climate blogger Joe Romm told Thomas Friedman of the *New York Times*: 'We created a way of raising standards of living that we can't possibly pass on to our children. We have been getting rich by depleting all our natural stocks – water, hydrocarbons, forests, rivers, fish and arable land – and not by generating renewable flows.'[15]

By the mid-1970s the critics had won. Concerns about limits to growth began to recede from public debate. Yet the report's findings continued to resonate in the burgeoning environmental movement. Indeed, *Limits to Growth* changed the language of environmental discourse and gave birth to the field of ecological economics where growth is the central focus. The Club of Rome report put in place the notion of renewable and non-renewable 'stocks' and 'flows' of natural resources. And these concepts set the stage for what we'll look at in the next chapter.

What are the limits of our energy and raw materials?

Can efficiency, producing more with less, solve our problems?

1 Darwin's original title was: *On the Origin of Species by Means of Natural Selection, or the Preservation of Favoured Races in the Struggle for Life.* **2** Herman Daly, *Beyond growth: the economics of sustainable development,* Beacon Press, 1996. **3, 4** Cited in Bill McKibbon, *Deep Economy,* Holt, 2008. **5** Brian Milner, 'Global outlook turns darker', *The Globe and Mail,* 9 Oct 2012. **6** Suzanne Daly, 'Spain Recoils as Its Hungry Forage Trash Bins for a Next Meal', *New York Times,* 24 Sept 2012. **7** Earth Policy Institute, www.earth-policy.org/data_highlights/2011/highlights18 **8** *Growth isn't possible,* New Economics Foundation, 2010. **9, 10** John Stuart Mill, *Principles of Political Economy with some of their Applications to Social Philosophy,* Book 4, 1848. **11** Frederick Soddy, *Wealth, Virtual Wealth and Debt: The Solution of the Economic Paradox,* Dutton, 1926. **12** Robert Skidelsky, *John Maynard Keynes, 1883-1946: Economist, Philosopher, Statesman,* Penguin, 2005. **13** Cited in Christian Kerschner, 'Economic de-growth vs steady-state economy', *Journal of Cleaner Production 18,* 2010. **14** Peter A Victor, *Managing Without Growth,* Edward Elgar, 2008. **15** Thomas L Friedman, 'The Inflection Is Near?', *New York Times,* 7 Mar 2009.

2 Sources, sinks and services

EF Schumacher laid out the idea of the Earth's 'natural capital' on which humanity depends. But those resources are being consumed faster with every passing year – and technological improvements and efficiency savings are utterly unable to keep pace. The Earth's sinks are now overflowing – and we are starting to pay a heavy price.

'The idea of unlimited growth... needs to be seriously questioned on at least two counts: the availability of basic resources and... the capacity of the environment to cope with the degree of interference implied.'

EF Schumacher

A year after *The Limits to Growth* appeared, a soft-spoken ex-economist from the British Coal Board, EF Schumacher released a slim volume of essays with a catchy title: *Small is Beautiful: economics as if people mattered*. The timing was right. The global economy was reeling in the wake of the 1973 OPEC 'oil crisis'. Oil-producing Arab nations had suddenly cut supply and jacked up the price of crude in retaliation for US support of Israel during the Yom Kippur War. Global commodity prices surged in tandem with oil. And three years earlier, in April 1970, the first Earth Day brought 20 million Americans to the streets. The environment was becoming a matter of growing public concern.

Schumacher's work was received as a blast of common sense, a lucid critique of Western economics that brought things sharply into focus. He wrote with passion and clarity about the environmental effects of economic growth, suggesting an alternative to the neoclassical paradigm grounded in what he called 'Buddhist Economics'. By that he meant an economics of consumption based on 'sufficiency', opportunities for people to participate in 'useful and fulfilling work' (which he called 'Right Livelihood' based on one of the requirements of Buddha's Noble Eightfold Path) and an engaged, active community marked by peace and co-operation. He called for human-scale, decentralized and 'appropriate technologies' as an alternative to a rapacious, dangerous and unjust global system. 'Ever-bigger machines, entailing ever-bigger concentrations of economic power and exerting ever-greater violence against the environment, do not represent progress: they are the denial of wisdom.'[1]

As Schumacher saw it, the human economic system must operate within, and be subject to, the constraints of the natural world. For him, this was the major failing of mainstream economics. It was in the end, he thought, a reflection of both human arrogance and human ignorance. 'Modern man [sic] does not experience himself as part of nature but as an outside force destined to dominate and conquer it. He even talks of a battle with nature, forgetting that if he won the battle he would find himself on the losing side.'

Schumacher was the first popular writer to introduce the concept of 'natural capital' to a wider audience. This was a kind of analytic *ju-jitsu* in which he used the language of economics to illustrate his core idea of the environmental limits to growth. In 'natural capital' he included all renewable and non-renewable resources, as well as all ecosystem services and systems – from the pollination of crops through the decomposition of wastes to the regulation of the global climate. Schumacher acknowledged the role of science and technology in creating human-made, 'sophisticated capital equipment' but noted that this is a small part of the overall capital on which we depend.

'Far larger is the capital provided by nature and not by man – and we do not even recognize it as such. This larger part is now being used up at an alarming rate and that is why it is an absurd and suicidal error to believe, and act on the belief, that the problem of production has been solved... The modern industrial system, with all its intellectual sophistication, consumes the very basis on which it has been erected... It lives on irreplaceable capital, which it treats as income.'

Since Schumacher first popularized the term, ecologists have embraced it, dividing the Earth's natural capital into three broad categories, all of which are critical to maintaining growth.

Sources

The first and most obvious category of 'sources' includes energy and the basic raw materials that are harvested from the planet and fed into the industrial machine. Energy, specifically oil, is the lifeblood of modern economies. Around 90 per cent of our energy comes from fossil fuels – coal, oil and natural gas.

Oil is number one, accounting for 35 per cent of the world's primary energy consumption.[2] Two-thirds of it goes towards transport – powering our trains, airplanes, cars, trucks, ocean freighters, speedboats and snowmobiles. Oil is also at the heart of modern industry, providing the energy and chemical feed stocks to churn out endless consumer goods, electronics, pharmaceuticals, construction materials, machine tools, scientific equipment, chemicals, clothing and myriad other items that mesh into the seamless system of production that now straddles the globe. Perhaps more vitally, petroleum is the energy source that powers modern agriculture. Oil provides chemical fertilizers, pesticides and herbicides while gasoline fuels farm machinery. Oil is also essential to the processing, packaging and distribution of foodstuffs. There is a direct correlation between economic growth and oil consumption. Faster growth requires more oil, lower growth less. That's why, in times of recession, when growth softens, demand for oil also falls. The same is true for other strategic metals and minerals like copper, iron, nickel, chromium, zinc, tin and manganese. Yet, like oil, the overall trend in the price of raw materials has been rising over the past decade.

When Dennis Meadows and his associates were building the original *Limits to Growth* model back in the early 1970s they were concerned that we would exhaust supplies of basic metals and other industrial raw materials within 50 years. That hasn't happened. The global economy has expanded 10-fold since then and mining corporations have ransacked countries from Brazil and Peru to Canada and Mongolia in search of strategic materials. Extraction technologies have become more sophisticated and exploration continues to expand at an ever-increasing rate to the remotest corners of the planet. In 2008, the weight

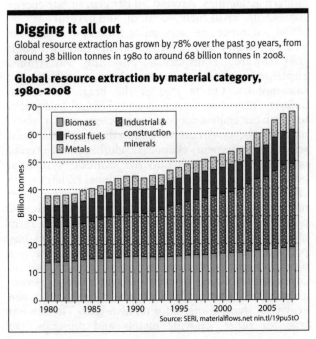

Digging it all out

Global resource extraction has grown by 78% over the past 30 years, from around 38 billion tonnes in 1980 to around 68 billion tonnes in 2008.

Global resource extraction by material category, 1980-2008

Source: SERI, materialflows.net nin.tl/19pu5tO

of all materials extracted and harvested around the world totaled 68 billion tonnes, nearly 25 kilograms a day for every person living on the planet. Global resource extraction has grown by nearly 80 per cent since 1980. The largest rise in per-capita consumption has occurred in the industrialized world.[3]

We have not bumped up against the limits of these strategic metals yet. But it would be imprudent to assume that supplies are limitless. If the rest of the world consumed copper, zinc, tin, chromium and silver at the same rate as the US, it is estimated that the global supply of those strategic metals would disappear in less than two decades.

A 2009 study highlighted by the Worldwatch Institute outlines broad-brush estimates of the availability of common metals based on current levels of consumption. Within the next century we will see major shortages of most basic raw materials as rich seams of ore are used up and new discoveries dwindle.[4] Existing stocks will also become more expensive to pry out of the ground as ore grades decline. Part of the problem will be real physical shortages, but equally important will be the price of energy used in extraction as oil prices inevitably creep upwards.

Mainstream economists, business leaders and many scientists place their hope in technology and human ingenuity. They look at the last century of scientific achievement and technological progress as just the beginning of more and better innovation. Why worry about running out of resources, they ask, when we can become more efficient by improving our technology?

Isn't technology an infinite resource? The short answer is, no. As Herman Daly writes: 'Improved technology means using the entropic flow [remember our entropy discussion from the last chapter] more efficiently, not reversing the direction of the flow. Efficiency is subject to thermodynamic limits. All existing and currently conceivable technologies function on an entropy gradient, converting low entropy into high entropy, in net terms.'[5]

The counter argument is that efficiency improvements – doing more with less – mean we don't need to worry about running out of raw materials. We can continue to have economic growth using less energy, fewer material inputs and fewer workers. (Don't ask what happened to full employment. Efficiency demands increased productivity and, if that means more labor-saving technology and fewer good jobs, then so be it. That is the price we must pay for growth.)

Indeed, these claims are not without precedent. Industry has made huge strides in efficiency in recent years. Across the world economies have become less 'energy intensive', driving down the amount of energy used to produce every unit of GDP. The US, for example, used 20,000 BTU (British Thermak Units) of energy in 1950 to produce one dollar of GDP. By 2008 that had been slashed to 8,500 BTU. In addition to technology 'fixes', economists have a strong faith in 'price signals' and 'substitution'.

Introductory economics textbooks say that if a resource becomes scarce then its price will rise to the point where users will look for a cheaper substitute. This might make sense in some instances. For example, if a bakery finds refined white sugar hard to source and too expensive then it might search for a cheaper alternative – honey, perhaps, or an artificial sweetener. But what works at the micro level may not work at the macro level. In the case of critical inputs, like oil, a substitute is not so easily available.

The Jevons Paradox

The notion that the economy can be 'de-coupled' from material inputs and so continue merrily down the growth pathway is dubious. This is largely due to a little-known hiccough called the Jevons Paradox or 'rebound effect'. In his 1865 book, *The Coal Question*, the British economist, W Stanley Jevons, posited that greater energy efficiency produces savings in the short run but in the long run results in higher energy use.

'It is a confusion of ideas to suppose that the economical use of fuel is equivalent to diminished consumption,' Jevons wrote. 'The very contrary is the truth.'

How can that be? Well, Jevons argued that just because we use energy (or raw materials) more efficiently doesn't mean we'll use less of them, especially in an economic system predicated on growth. The Jevons paradox, in a nutshell, says that the benefits of increased technical efficiency are inevitably swamped by increased consumption. Improvements in efficiency translate into lower prices in the short term, which in turn trigger higher consumption. You see this 'rebound effect' when the price of gasoline falls and people drive their cars more. Or when savings on energy-efficient light bulbs and appliances are used to buy a new flat-screen TV or another household gadget.

We're caught in a bind. Ramping up GDP without improving technological efficiency leads to more resource inputs, more energy consumed and environmental damage. Yet improving efficiency triggers more growth – which leads to the same end. Total resource consumption grows even while efficiency improves. Between 1970 and 2000, rich countries saw impressive gains in energy efficiency of up to 40 per cent. But average improvements of two per cent a year were eclipsed by growth rates of three per cent a year or more.

In one study cited by the New Economics Foundation (NEF), environmental economist Toyoaki Washida found a significant 'rebound effect' in the Japanese economy that swallowed 35-70 per cent of the efficiency savings.[6] According to NEF, 'even if technological energy efficiency and the uptake of new, more efficient devices increased by 50 per cent over the next

20-30 years with GDP rising by a conservative 2.5 per cent, within 25 years we'd be back where we are now.'

Other researchers confirm that growth eventually swamps efficiency improvements. In a study of the material outflows of five industrial nations, the World Resources Institute found that industrial economies are becoming more efficient in their use of materials, but that waste generation also continues to increase. 'Even as decoupling between economic growth and resource throughput occurred on a per-capita and per-unit GDP basis, however, overall resource use and waste flows continued to grow. *We found no evidence of an absolute reduction in resource throughput.*'[7]

The chart below shows exactly that. Even though 'material intensity' (the volume of materials consumed per unit of GDP) has been decreasing since 1980, the total volume of materials extracted continues to increase. We are using fewer resources more efficiently.

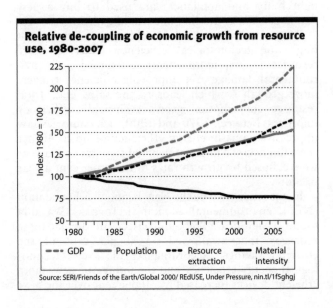

Relative de-coupling of economic growth from resource use, 1980-2007

Index: 1980 = 100

- - - GDP   — Population   ● ● ● Resource extraction   ━━ Material intensity

Source: SERI/Friends of the Earth/Global 2000/ REdUSE, Under Pressure, nin.tl/1f5ghgj

But it makes little difference if growth and population continue to rise.

This does not mean efficiency improvements are a second-tier priority, as some free market boosters suggest. Critics like the Washington-based Institute for Energy Research (funded by, among others, ExxonMobil Corporation and billionaire Tea Party supporters, the Koch brothers) maintain that the market must be left on its own and that efficiency should not be enforced by government regulation. Directing energy policy through regulation is a 'folly', the Institute says. 'Instead of forcing more energy-efficiency requirements on American consumers, policy-makers and government regulators should allow market prices and disruptive innovations to guide energy use.'[8]

But it's not the goal that is wobbly, it's the context. Efficiency improvements are necessary – but not sufficient. It's the growth that negates the efficiency savings that is the real issue.

Growth optimists also boast that physical resource limits are irrelevant in our new knowledge-based economy. As economies 'mature' and shift from production to finance, insurance and real estate (the so-called FIRE sector), engineering, education and other services, there will be less need for raw materials. As the economy 'dematerializes' we will continue to grow as our workplaces and homes become greener and cleaner. Unfortunately, there is little evidence of this happening. For the most part advanced industrial economies have simply shifted production overseas where labor costs are cheaper, taxes less burdensome and environmental regulations weak or non-existent. So, as Western countries 'offload' production of real goods overseas, the global pollution load actually increases.

High-end service jobs also generally pay more, which inevitably means more consumption. But, while resource-intensive manufacturing has relocated abroad, we in the West are no less addicted to our 'stuff' – hi-tech electronic gadgets, sprawling suburbs, new cars and cheap flights to warm places. As our consumption increases, we are merely 'outsourcing' the problem. Out of sight, out of mind. We are still chomping through tons of raw materials. It's just that now the 'throughput' is halfway around the globe. All we see are the final results on display in the local mall. As University of British Columbia ecologist William Rees notes: 'High-income service employees therefore have much larger per-capita ecological footprints than workers in the basic economy; those countries with the largest high-end service sectors have the largest national eco-footprints.'

The overflowing sinks

What goes into the maw of the growth machine must eventually come out the other end as waste. The waste comes in many forms – from household garbage, plastic bottles and construction refuse to slaughterhouse offal, toxic tailings, noxious gases and pesticide residues. All of these find their way into one of Planet Earth's natural 'sinks': the air, the water or the land. Until the last 50 years or so this was not really a problem. Mother Nature could take just about anything we could throw at her. All that has changed. Today the absorptive and assimilative capacities of the Earth can no longer handle the Niagara-like torrents of waste we are disgorging.

The 'sinks' are overflowing. The evidence is clear wherever we turn as our rapacious global economy hits the limits. All major ecosystems are being degraded at an astonishing speed. It's a depressing litany that includes the ransacking of ocean fisheries (12 of the world's 13 major fisheries are now severely depleted); the continued destruction of tropical rainforests; fertile soils salted with agro-chemicals and converted to industrial agriculture; increasing desertification; the destruction of wilderness; species extinction and the erosion of biodiversity. The list goes on.

Take the case of synthetic chemicals – the hazards of which Rachel Carson, whose pioneering 1962 book, *Silent Spring*, is credited with launching the environmental movement, first raised over 50 years ago. We continue to pump millions of tons of deadly chemicals into the environment every year and the damage both to humans and nature is no longer in doubt. We are living in a deadly stew of toxins, most of which did not exist before modern chemistry was born in the crucible of World War Two.

There are more than 80,000 chemicals in industrial production today, with hundreds added each year. Few have been tested for their effect on human health or the environment. And, critically, there is almost no knowledge of how chemicals interact with each other. When the Toxic Substances Control Act (TSCA) was passed in the US in 1976, more than 62,000 chemicals were 'grandfathered' into the market – in other words, no testing, no questions asked. According to investigative journalist Mark Schapiro, these included highly toxic substances such as ethyl benzene, a widely used industrial solvent suspected of being a potent neurotoxin; whole families of synthetic plastics that are potential carcinogens and endocrine disrupters; and thousands of other substances for which there was little or no information. The Environmental Protection Agency (EPA) admits that 95 per cent of all chemicals have not undergone even minimal testing for toxicity. In the European Union it's estimated that two-thirds of the 30,000 most commonly used chemicals have not been vetted. According to Schapiro, the EPA had banned just five chemicals in the quarter-century prior to 2007.[9] All of us live with this toxic burden. But the poor, the marginalized, and the people of color, those who are cheek-by-jowl with industrial plants, suffer the most.

Rachel Carson would have been outraged but not surprised. 'The chemical war is never won,' she wrote in *Silent Spring*, 'and all life is caught in its violent crossfire.' It was Carson who first promoted the notion of ecology, the complex web that binds human life to the natural world. 'The serious student of earth history knows that neither life nor the physical world that supports it exists in little isolated compartments... harmful substances released into the environment return in time to create problems for mankind [sic]... We cannot think of the living organism alone; nor can we think of the physical environment as a separate entity. The two exist together, each acting on the other to form an ecological complex or ecosystem.'[10]

As humankind pushes ever deeper into the most remote areas of the globe, expanding our industrial production and consumer habits, we threaten natural systems and sully the last remnants of wilderness left on our 'full' planet. ATVs (all terrain vehicles) thunder across alpine meadows deep in the Rocky Mountains. Seismic lines crisscross the high Arctic. Cattle ranches and industrial-scale soy farms replace dense, tropical forests in the Brazilian Amazon, displacing native peoples and destroying a unique pharmacological treasure trove. Nearly a fifth of Brazil's tropical forests have been logged over the past four decades – more than in the previous 450 years since European contact. It is estimated than another 20 per cent may be lost in the next decade.

As a result of habitat destruction, hunting, invasion by alien species, disease and climate change, the speed of global extinction is accelerating. There are now more than 17,000 plants and animals at risk, according to the International Union for Conservation of Nature (IUCN). This Swiss NGO's Red List of endangered species records that 25 per cent of all invertebrates, 20 per cent of mammals, half of all primates, one in eight birds, a third of all amphibians and half of all turtles face extinction. When the IUCN first released figures in 2004, it noted that we are losing species 100-1,000 times faster than the normal 'background' rate suggested by fossil records before humans were around. Between a third and a half of all terrestrial species are expected to die out over the next 200 years if nothing is done to stop habitat destruction. Scientists generally put the normal extinction rate at about one species every four years. Harvard's EO Wilson, one of the world's most eminent biologists, has predicted the rate of species extinction could reach 10,000 times the 'background' rate in the next 20 years.

The Anthropocene and nature's services

The destructive impact of human activity on the Earth has become so pervasive that ecologists now suggest that the previous geological era has ended and we have entered a new age: the Anthropocene. Paul Crutzen, a Nobel-prize winning Dutch chemist, coined the word in 2000. Crutzen was attending a scientific conference where the chair kept referring to the Holocene, the period that started at the end of the last ice age nearly 12,000 years ago. 'Let's stop it. We are no longer in the Holocene. We are in the Anthropocene,' Crutzen recalls blurting out. 'Well, it was quiet in the room for a while.' When the group took a coffee break, the Anthropocene was the main topic of conversation.[11] No wonder. No other species has had the dubious distinction of defining a geological era by its activities. According to the Royal Society, the Anthropocene is a 'vivid expression of the degree of environmental change on planet Earth'. We have laid down a trail, left our mark, indelibly, on ice cores in the Antarctic and in new layers of sedimentary rock being laid on the ocean floor.

Two recent events highlight the threat that economic growth poses to 'ecosystem services', the natural cycles and systems that make our planet green, clean and habitable. We mentioned Fritz Schumacher's inclusion of these 'services' in the phrase 'natural capital'. But let me say a little more about these gifts that nature bestows on us and which we mostly take for granted. They include those fundamental processes that lurk in the background of our daily lives – the water cycle, photosynthesis, pollination, flood control, the decomposition of wastes and, ultimately, the regulation of the global climate. Unfortunately, both the terms 'natural capital' and 'ecosystem services' adopt the dry language of economics to interpret the richness and mystery of nature. Nonetheless, they are useful, if mechanistic, shorthand to counter the prejudices of mainstream economics, in which the environment has never been treated as more than an 'externality'. This of course is nonsense. Nature is not external; it is fundamental. The human economy is not a self-contained system. It is a product of human culture and human culture is uniquely, delicately, nested in the natural systems of the biosphere.

So let's look now at those three examples of the erosion of ecosystem services by exponential growth.

When NASA released satellite photos of the Greenland ice sheet, taken four days apart, in July 2012, the contrast between the two images could not have been starker. An unusual Arctic heat wave had melted a vast expanse of surface ice; approximately 97 per cent of it had thawed in less than a week. We're talking about the surface here. The ice did not disappear. It's almost two miles thick in places so it will take decades to melt to bare earth. But Greenland's ice sheet is dwindling, undeniably, a little more with each passing year. About four times more ice melted in the summer of 2012 than in the 10 previous years. The Intergovernmental Panel on Climate Change (IPCC), a UN-mandated grouping of the world's most eminent climate scientists, warns that if Greenland's ice sheet were to melt completely it would raise sea levels by 7.5 meters.

Back in 2007 the IPCC said that we would not see ice-free summers in the Arctic for another century. That now looks wildly optimistic. Things are changing even more quickly than forecast. A month after the NASA Greenland photo, researchers using data from the European Space Agency's satellite corroborated the NASA findings for the Arctic as a whole. The Polar ice cap, too, had melted at an unprecedented rate – in total more than 11.7 million square kilometers, 22 per cent more than average. Scientists now predict an ice-free Arctic summer within 20 years. 'This is staggering,' Cambridge University sea-ice researcher Nick Toberg told *The Guardian*. 'It's disturbing, scary that we have physically changed the face of the planet.'[12] Studies show that 60-95 per cent of the melting of Arctic ice between 1953 and 2011 was due to human activity. There is little doubt that human-induced global warming has been more extreme in the far north. The area has been heating up about twice as fast as the rest of the world.

The summer of 2012 also saw shocking news from the tropics, where the world's coral reefs are under increasing threat. If you've floated, awestruck, above a living reef in the Caribbean, off the coast of Queensland or elsewhere, you'll have witnessed the exquisite beauty and amazing bounty of tropical coral reefs. And if you haven't actually swum near a reef you'll have seen film or photos of these natural treasures. Coral reefs are a classic ecosystem service. They are home to a quarter of all marine species. They protect islands and coasts from wind-whipped seas. They draw tens of thousands of tourists and they provide a rich fishery for millions. Now, as a result of rising greenhouse gas emissions and increased acidification, the reefs are dying. A report from the Global Coral Reef Monitoring Network, compiled by 36 scientists from 18 countries, found that only 8 per cent of reefs in the Caribbean have live coral cover compared to 50 per cent in the 1970s. A similar study from the World Resources Institute found that 75 per cent of all Caribbean reefs and more than 95 per cent of those in Southeast Asia were in danger. Scientists now predict that all coral reefs will suffer 'long-term degradation' by 2030.

Another recent study gives a broader framework to the notion of long-term degradation. In the September 2009 issue of the journal *Nature*, Swedish researcher Johan Rockström and his colleagues devised a system of 'planetary boundaries' which they said defined a 'safe operating space for humanity'.[13] They concluded that we have already transgressed three of the boundaries – climate change, biodiversity loss and interference with the nitrogen cycle. And we are poised on the threshold of four more – global freshwater consumption; the conversion of virgin land to agriculture; ocean acidification; and interference with the global phosphorous cycle. Moreover, these boundaries overlap. They are contingent and connected so that a change in one may shade into another, bringing unforeseen consequences. Like the 'butterfly effect' in chaos theory, when seemingly trivial events may change the course of history, Rockström underlined the inter-connectedness of the global environment, where 'significant land-use changes in the Amazon could influence water resources as far away as Tibet' or 'transgressing the nitrogen-phosphorus boundary can erode the resilience of some marine ecosystems, potentially reducing their capacity to absorb CO_2 and thus affecting the climate boundary'. What's clear is that by exceeding these planetary boundaries we're setting ourselves up for catastrophic environmental change. We don't have 'the luxury of concentrating our efforts on any one of them', the report notes. And we can't continue on our current path 'without significantly eroding the resilience of major components' of the planet's delicate natural systems.

The news from the Arctic, from the world's tropical reefs, and from Johan Rockström's research, is confirmation, if any was needed, of the UN Millennium Ecosystem Assessment, a collaborative work of more than 10,000 scientists released in 2005. The UN found that 60 per cent of 'ecosystem services' were being degraded or used unsustainably. Those included 'fresh water, capture fisheries, air and water purification and the regulation of regional and local climate'. Human activity is putting such a heavy strain on the natural functions of the Earth, the report warned, 'that the ability of the planet's ecosystems to sustain human endeavor can no longer be taken for granted.'

Growth boosters maintain that we need more growth, not less, to heal the global environment. They point to the enormously successful 'end of pipe' solutions to pollution adopted by industrial countries over the past 50 years. Without growth and the resulting boost in wealth, they argue, we would never have been able to afford to clean up England's River Thames or North America's Great Lakes, ban DDT and leaded fuels, or phase out chlorofluorocarbons (CFCs). This phenomenon is based on the work of Simon Kuznets, the father of econometrics and a leading US economist who pioneered the concept of GDP back in the 1930s. Kuznets argued that the path of economic development followed an inverted 'U'. In the initial stages, as a country industrializes and gets richer, inequality also increases until a rising level of average income tips the balance and wealth begins to trickle down to the poor, ushering in an era of greater equality. This same logic has been applied to the environmental damage caused by growth – things must get worse before they get better. There is a grain of truth in this analysis. Hungry people do not make good environmental stewards. And greater wealth can bring both improved pollution-fighting technologies and leisure time to appreciate and understand the value of the natural world. But while the logic may apply to specific cases it ignores the big picture. As we have seen, the overall trend is one of steep decline.

Herman Daly once said that he would accept the possibility of infinite growth when his fellow economists could demonstrate that the earth itself could grow at a commensurate rate. This has not yet happened. The uncomfortable truth is that the physical resources of the biosphere are finite. We're not approaching the ecological limits to growth; we're past them. And in the process we're fouling the globe with our wastes and threatening the natural systems on which humanity and all other species depend, as the next chapter explains.

1 EF Schumacher, *Small is Beautiful, 25 years later with commentaries*, Hartley & Marks, Vancouver, 1999. 2 Dahr Jamail, 'Oil: In perpetuity no more', *Al Jazeera*, 21 Feb 2012. 3 *Under Pressure: How our material consumption threatens the planet's water resources*, Global 2000/SERI, http://seri.at/wp-content/uploads/2011/11/Under_Pressure_Nov1111.pdf 4 Gary Gardner, 'Materials Use Up', *Vital Signs 2011*, Worldwatch Institute, 2011. 5 Herman Daly, *Steady State Economics*, Earthscan, 1992. 6 *Growth isn't possible*, New Economics Foundation, 2010. 7 Cited in Peter A Victor, *Managing Without Growth*, Elgar, 2008. 8 'Energy efficiency mandates have rebound effect', Institute for Energy Research, 12 Jul 2012. 9 Mark Schapiro, *Exposed: the toxic chemistry of everyday products*, Chelsea Green, 2008. 10 Rachel Carson, *Silent Spring*, Houghton-Mifflin, 1962. 11 Elizabeth Kolbert, 'Age of Man', *National Geographic*, Mar 2011. 12 John Vidal, 'The staggering decline of sea ice at the frontline of climate change,' *The Guardian*, 21 Sep 2012. 13 www.nature.com

3 Climate change and carbon footprints

Ever more violent storms, heat waves and floods are leading even mainstream economists and insurance companies to join the voices warning about climate change. The evidence is irresistible that we are living beyond our means – but energy corporations and governments are still covering their ears.

'Continued exploitation of all fossil fuels on Earth threatens not only the other millions of species on the planet but also the survival of humanity itself – and the time is shorter than we thought.'

James Hansen

Where I live, in eastern Canada, the winter of 2011/2012 was a bust. There was the odd dusting of snow and a few normal cold days but generally it was a non-event. Summer arrived in Toronto in late March with five consecutive days of 20-degree heat. Fruit trees were forced into bloom weeks earlier than usual. Outdoor patios were filled with eager sun worshippers and people in the streets wore relaxed smiles. It was strangely liberating, as the sudden arrival of a warm spring always is. But it was also unsettling – more like Tennessee or Kentucky than southern Ontario.

But, of course, these days we're not alone. This kind of 'extreme weather event', as the climatologists like to say, is everywhere more the norm than the exception. There is little doubt that the global climate is changing, that our weather is becoming more unpredictable and that the planet is heating up. A recent study commissioned by the Toronto Environment Office predicts that the city will sweat through five times as many 'heat waves' 30 years from now. The number of days above 30°C will triple to 66 and the number of days the humidex (temperature plus humidity) hits 40°C will jump from 9 to 39.[1] 'Imagine a summer where for two months the temperature does not go below 30°C,' environmental activist Franz Hartmann told the *Toronto Star*. 'If that were to happen tomorrow there would probably be a significant number of deaths. Our electricity infrastructure would fail... and who knows what else would happen to the urban infrastructure? I'm not sure that the city or this administration is taking any of this stuff seriously.'[2]

Who *is* taking this stuff seriously? Not the major oil companies or the rest of the fossil-fuel industry it seems – self-interest is a powerful aid to wilful blindness. But some astute politicians and many ordinary citizens are beginning to take note. After Hurricane Sandy slammed into the US eastern seaboard in October 2012, causing billions of dollars' worth of damage, widespread flooding and 40,000 homeless, New York City's one-per-cent mayor, Michael Bloomberg, made his position clear. 'Our climate is changing,' he commented via Twitter. 'And while the increase in extreme weather we have experienced in NYC and around the world may or may not be the result of it, the risk that it may be – given the devastation it is wreaking – should be enough to compel all elected leaders to take immediate action.' The cover lines of the usually pro-corporate, Bloomberg-owned, *Businessweek* were more pointed: 'It's global warming, stupid', the magazine blared. The state's governor (and possible future Democratic presidential candidate) Andrew Cuomo agreed. Citing a $33-billion price tag for Hurricane Sandy, Cuomo said: 'Anyone who thinks there is not dramatic change in weather patterns is denying reality. We have a new reality and old systems.'

The data speaks for itself. Average global temperatures have slowly but steadily warmed since the 1880s, as forests have been cleared and oil-powered transport

A sign that the business and political establishment is finally waking up to the dangers of climate change: the front cover of *Bloomberg Businessweek* from 5-11 November 2012.

and industry have spread, ineluctably, to the farthest corners of the planet. The end of the 19th century was the beginning of the 'modern record'. From that point on, weather stations could provide enough information to compare global temperatures. As greenhouse-gas emissions rose, temperatures climbed, especially from the mid-1970s onwards. Recent analysis from NASA's Goddard Institute for Space Studies (GISS) in New York shows that the average global surface temperature in 2011 was 0.51°C warmer than in the mid-20th century and the ninth warmest since 1880. The warming trend continues. Nine of the ten warmest years have occurred since the year 2000, with 2010 being the warmest year on record. (The temperature analysis produced at GISS is based on data from more than 1,000 meteorological stations around the world as well as satellite observations of sea surface temperature and Antarctic research station measurements.)

Higher temperatures today are largely sustained by increased atmospheric concentrations of greenhouse gases, especially carbon dioxide (CO_2). These gases absorb and hold the sun's infrared radiation, most of which usually bounces off the Earth and escapes into space. As more greenhouse gases accumulate, they trap more energy, which in turn leads to higher temperatures. Scientists can measure the amount of carbon dioxide in the atmosphere. They know it was about 285 parts per million (ppm) in 1880, when the GISS global temperature record begins. By 1960, the concentration had risen to 315 ppm. Today, CO_2 levels top 400 ppm and continue to rise by about 2 ppm every year. So far the 'greenhouse effect' from this extra CO_2 has raised the average temperature of the planet by 0.8°C. In 2009, 167 countries signed the

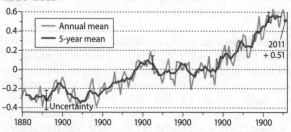

An ever warmer world

Nine of the 10 warmest years since 1880 have occurred since 2000. From 2000-2010 the Earth experienced sustained higher temperatures than in any decade during the 20th century. As CO_2 levels continue to rise, long-term temperatures will also continue to increase.

Global temperature difference in degrees Celsius, 1880-2010

(Data: NASA Goddard Institute for Space Studies. Image: NASA Earth Observatory, Robert Simmon)

Copenhagen Accord, pledging a 'deep cut in global emissions… to hold the increase in global temperature below two degrees Celsius.'

So that's the bottom line: two degrees or less.

Climate warnings go mainstream

James Hansen, the director of GISS and one of the world's most respected climate scientists, first sounded the public alarm about global warming back in 1998. More than a decade later, the science is irrefutable. The weight of evidence continues to mount and Hansen's voice has been joined by a growing chorus. Concern about climate change is no longer confined to academics, crusading scientists or environmentalists.

Main greenhouse gases

Carbon dioxide (CO_2)

The number-one greenhouse gas emitted by human activities, this is responsible for 85% of global warming since the year 2000. The amount of CO_2 in the atmosphere reached 390.9 parts per million (ppm) in 2011 according to the World Meteorological Organization (WMO), 140% above pre-industrial levels of 280 ppm. The concentration of CO_2 is increasing by 2 ppm every year.

Methane (CH_4)

Methane is the second most powerful greenhouse gas. About 40% comes from natural sources (bubbling up from wetlands and swamps) while 60% stems from human activities – from farting livestock and burning crop residues to rotting garbage and the flaring of waste natural gas. The WMO says methane reached a new high of 1813 parts per billion (ppb) in 2011, 259% above pre-industrial levels.

Nitrous oxide (N_2O)

N_2O packs a global-warming punch 298 times greater than CO_2 and destroys the ozone layer to boot. Like CH_4, 60% of nitrous oxide is due to human sources and 40% to natural sources. It comes from the bacterial breakdown of nitrogen in soil and in the oceans. But it is also a by-product of sewage treatment, animal manure and modern soil-management techniques. The atmospheric concentration of N_2O was 324.2 ppb in 2011, more than 120% of the pre-industrial level. ■

Critics are beginning to emerge from the corporate world, too, especially from the accounting and insurance industries. In a recent report titled 'Too late for two degrees?' PricewaterhouseCoopers (PwC), the world's biggest accounting firm (with 2011 revenues of $29.2 billion), warns that we've already passed 'a critical threshold' and that we may be looking at increases of 4-6°C in the next century. The report notes that the 2011 rate of *improvement* in carbon intensity (the carbon produced per unit of economic output) was 0.8 per cent but emphasizes that even if we double that we'll still wind up with six degrees of warming. To give ourselves more than a 50-per-cent chance of avoiding two degrees will require a six-fold improvement in our rate of decarbonization. It's worth noting that the 4-6°C rise we're headed for will leave the world hotter than at any time in the last 30 million years.

'We have to reduce emissions by 5.1 per cent per year, every year, from now until 2050,' PwC's Jonathan Grant said. 'It looks very unlikely that we will be able to achieve these targets.' The report concludes that 'businesses, governments and communities across the world need to plan for a warming world – not just 2°C, but 4°C and, at our current rates, 6°C.' Grant is right in that we do need to 'plan for a warming world'. That is inevitable. Even if we limit the temperature rise to 2°C, the lingering effect of accumulated carbon in the atmosphere will contribute to climate instability for decades. For all its plain speaking, the PricewaterhouseCoopers report fails to connect the spiraling levels of carbon with the worldwide pursuit of economic growth. The unchallenged assumption here is that 'decarbonization' can stem the tide in a world addicted to steady increases in GDP. Given what we know about the propensity of growth to eclipse gains in efficiency, the notion that this is our best escape route seems misguided at best.

Yet another study, this time from the World Bank, was released in advance of the UN-sponsored climate talks in Doha in November 2012 and drew similar conclusions.[3] The Bank's researchers confirm that we are *en route* to a 4°C warmer world by the end of the century, leading to average summer temperatures about 6°C higher in North Africa, the Mediterranean, the Middle East and North America. Current CO_2 emission reduction pledges won't make much difference. All regions of the world will suffer from climate change but poor countries will suffer most.

Pumped-up CO_2 levels will trigger a 150-per-cent rise in ocean acidification by 2100, an event 'unparalleled in Earth's history'. This will not only put an end to the world's coral reefs, it will also be the *coup de grâce* for global fish stocks. (More than a billion people today depend on fish as their main source of protein.) The report also rejects a 'zero-sum' approach to the effect of climate change on global food production – in other words, the notion that some areas will gain and others will lose but that overall things will more or less break even. 'Results suggest instead a rapidly rising risk of crop-yield reductions as the world warms.'

The World Bank report also recognized the importance of 'tipping points', a concept that scientists have stressed for decades. The point is that climate change does not progress in a predictable, linear fashion – so the dangers may in fact be understated. Things can speed up without warning as 'feedback loops' magnify change. The 'albedo' effect is one example: when sea ice melts, the darker water absorbs more heat, which accelerates the melting, which in turn leads to more open ocean and more melting. Once the sea ice disappears and rising temperatures start to thaw the Arctic permafrost, we may witness the release of millions of tonnes of trapped methane, a much more potent greenhouse gas than carbon dioxide. That 'feedback loop' could lead to even more rapid and severe climate change. Another tipping point would be a 'large-scale Amazon dieback, drastically affecting ecosystems, rivers, agriculture, energy production and livelihoods in an almost continental scale' which would add 'substantially to 21st-century global warming'.

Yet the irony is that the World Bank refuses to 'walk the talk'. Its policies are still tilted in favor of fossil fuels, thus cranking up the thermostat even as it calls for 'turning down the heat'. It is a major funder of coal, oil and gas projects around the world. In 2010, the Bank loaned South Africa $3.75 billion to build a massive 4.8-gigawatt coal-fired power plant and spent a total of $4.4 billion on coal projects that year. The Jubilee South Asia Pacific Movement on Debt and Development says the World Bank is 'tainted by a history of financing projects that produce or heavily use fossil fuels' – the Bank has sunk more than $20 billion into fossil-fuel projects in the Asia Pacific region since the year 2000.

In 2010, more than 90 NGOs and activist groups sent an open letter to UN climate chief Christiana Figueres, protesting the World Bank's role in the Green Climate Fund, which is meant to help fund low-emissions development in the Global South.

> *In spite of the climate and economic crises, the World Bank continues to finance fossil fuel projects at an alarming rate, promote false solutions to the climate crisis, and use funding instruments that increase the indebtedness of developing countries. Thus, the World Bank is not suited to advise in the design of a fund that must ensure fair and effective long-term financing based on the principles of environmental integrity, equity, sustainable development, and democracy.*[4]

So good marks for analysis but not so good for performance.

The Bank's warning coincided with the release of the 2012 'Emissions Gap Report' from the UN Environment Programme (UNEP). The UNEP document is equally stark, suggesting that even if the most ambitious emission reduction targets are met it will still not be enough to avoid a two-degree hike this century. At the launch of the report, UNEP's chief scientist Joseph Alcamo told journalists: 'By 2030 we need to be 25 per cent below current global emissions and in 2050 we need to cut more than half of the current global emissions level. The scientists are telling us that if we are to stay on the path to limit warming to 2°C we need global emissions to peak before 2020. Current global emissions are already more than 10 per cent higher than the level annual emissions should be at in 2020 to stay within the recommended limit of warming.'

The poor bear the brunt

Across large swaths of the developing world millions of people are already struggling to adapt to deadly, unpredictable weather patterns. In a two-year research project examining the effects of climate change on rural communities in Africa, the Irish relief agency, Trocaire, found villagers wracked by food insecurity, migration, conflicts over resources and increased disease as a result of climate change.

In the Tharaka district of central Kenya, researchers found that annual rainfall has not only dropped by 15 per cent over the last 40 years but also no longer comes when it's most needed. At the same time the average temperature has increased. Because rain is now erratic and unpredictable, farming is more difficult. Crops are failing, animals are dying and hunger is on the rise. A generation ago, the average family in Tharaka owned 20 cattle and 50 goats. Today, that's dwindled to two cattle and five goats. More than 65 per cent of the region's 130,000 people now live in absolute poverty.

Trocaire's director, Justin Kilcullen, says people are trying to adapt but the odds are stacked against them. 'To buy drought-resistant seeds and irrigation equipment, they need money,' Kilcullen wrote in the *Irish Times*. 'Yet, as crops fail and animals die, they are becoming poorer, locked in a downward cycle. They are rightly anxious about where this is leading them. As one Tharaka farmer told me last year: "We used to know when the rain would come but now it is so unpredictable. Most of the time it does not come at all. When we should have rain, we instead have clear, blue sky. How can we grow food? How can we live?"'[5]

That question is being asked by more and more citizens across the developing world. In Africa alone, it is projected that by 2020 between 75 and 250 million people will face increased water stress as a result of climate change and in some countries agricultural yields could fall by up to 50 per cent. How this might heighten regional tensions and spark future conflict is anyone's guess. But the odds are that the changes won't be for the better. There is already ample evidence that ethnic clashes, religious violence and criminality are being fueled by climate change. Take the case of Afghanistan, where a period of prolonged drought has overlapped with the NATO occupation and the military drive to topple the Taliban. The response of Afghan farmers to the drought has been to plant more opium poppies, which are drought tolerant and can survive on less than a fifth of the water that wheat needs. The Taliban defends the right to grow opium, mainly because taxes on the lucrative crop help support their fight against the US-led invasion. The dismal link between violence, militarism and climate change is evident.

Meanwhile, in Italy and other Mediterranean areas, shifting rainfall patterns have increased flooding and threaten to alter patterns of food production. The Mediterranean Sea has warmed by almost two degrees over the past 20 years, which means that when Atlantic weather fronts move in they siphon up more moisture and more heat. That in turn triggers violent storms and torrential rain. According to Italian meteorologist Mario Giuliacci: 'An average of 80 mm of rain should fall in Italy in November. In the last 40 years it has gone over 100 mm 11 times, seven of which are since 1999.' The upshot? The country's climate is slowly changing, 'with drier summers and violent rains in winter, becoming more like North Africa'. Here's the kicker: in 2012 Sicily produced its first crop of bananas.[6]

The most serious humanitarian concern may be the waves of refugees driven from their homes by pounding storms, heat waves, wildfires, droughts and floods as climate change intensifies. In 2009 the UK-based Environmental Justice Foundation (EJF) estimated that 26 million people had already been forced to move due to climate change, and predicted that the figure could balloon to 150 million by 2050. The EJF claims that more than half a billion people, around seven per cent of the world's population, could be at risk.

The ultimate limit to growth

This much we know. The ability of the atmosphere to absorb carbon dioxide and its impact on the global climate is the ultimate limit to growth. There is a resounding consensus that, to avoid catastrophic consequences of the kind we've been describing, we can't raise the earth's average temperature by more than two degrees. Since the middle of the last century the world economy has grown more than five times and we've raised the average temperature by just under 0.8 degrees. If economic growth continues at more or less the same rate, the global economy will be 80 times bigger in 2100 than it was in 1950. As Tim Jackson notes in a report for Britain's Sustainable Development Commission, this ramping up of global economic activity has no historical precedent. 'It's totally at odds with our scientific knowledge of the finite resource base and the fragile ecology on which we depend for survival.'[7]

So how is it that we have reached such an impasse? In March 2012, the London-based Carbon Tracker Initiative (CTI) published a report called 'Unburnable Carbon – Are the world's financial markets carrying a carbon bubble?', which looked at the earth's 'carbon budget' from an investor's standpoint. The two central questions were simple, even if assembling the data was not.

How much carbon can we afford to dump into the atmosphere before we hit the wall? And how much carbon is there in the proven fossil-fuel reserves (coal, oil and gas) of the companies and countries that run the show? The group found that the most sophisticated climate simulation models put our carbon budget at 886 gigatonnes of carbon dioxide for the half century from 2000-2050 (1 gigatonne = 1,000,000,000 tonnes). That's the total we can add to the atmosphere without pushing past the two-degree limit. They also noted that by 2011 the world had already used a third of that figure, leaving just 565 gigatonnes to add before the middle of this century – and, with emission rates growing by three per cent a year, it will take less than 20 years to eat up those 565 gigatonnes.

But CTI also did some hard number crunching. They trawled through mountains of data and were able to put a number on the total proven reserves owned by private and public companies and governments. And they asked, more critically: what would happen if you burned it all? The answer – 2,795 gigatonnes of CO_2 would be added to the atmosphere. In other words, there is five times more coal, oil and gas in proven reserves in the ground than we can afford to burn.

The bottom line, says CTI, is that 'only 20 per cent of the total reserves can be burned unabated, leaving up to 80 per cent of assets technically unburnable'. So what does this mean for investors? The CTI analysts note that the 'conventional wisdom' is that all listed reserves will be exploited and burned. But, they say, the fact that a significant proportion of reserves will need to stay in the ground imposes a 'carbon constraint' – a *de facto* 'reduction in demand threatening a reduction in the value of these assets'. In other words, if governments ever get serious about putting a price on carbon, there will be more risk and less potential return on investment. Not what the markets like to hear. Instead, CTI argues for a 'rebalancing' to prevent the bursting of this 'carbon bubble'. Prudent investors are advised to reduce their exposure, to hedge their bets by shifting funds to alternative energy companies.

This is not a message the oil companies or major petro-states want to hear. And no wonder. It directly undermines the whole premise on which their market value and profitability is based. If 80 per cent of proven reserves eventually have to stay in the ground, that would mean 'writing off $20 trillion in assets' according to climate activist and journalist Bill McKibben. Not something the fossil-fuel giants are likely to do without a battle. Follow the money. That's the clue. The whole fossil-fuel edifice is built on the promise of future profits. As McKibben argues, the coal, oil and gas may still be 'technically in the ground' but as far as the companies are concerned it's already been dug up and stockpiled, written into their business plan. 'It's figured into share prices, companies are borrowing money against it, and nations are basing their budgets on the presumed returns from their patrimony. It explains why the big fossil-fuel companies have fought so hard to prevent the regulation of carbon dioxide – those reserves are their primary asset, the holding that gives their companies their value.'[8]

In any case, it's no secret that the fossil-fuel industry already has plenty of help getting its product to market. According to the Global Subsidies Initiative and the International Energy Agency (IEA), governments around the world subsidized fossil fuels to the tune of $623 billion in 2011: $100 billion for production and $523 billion for consumption. The IEA says eliminating subsidies on consumption by 2020 would cut CO_2 emissions by nearly two gigatonnes. That's like removing 350 million cars from the roads. Using public funds to support one of the most profitable industries in the world seems wrong-headed to say the least, given that the top five oil companies (Royal Dutch Shell, ExxonMobil, BP, Chevron and ConocoPhillips) made $137 billion in profits in 2012.[9]

This obvious denial of biophysical realities by fossil-fuel lobbyists and their supporters is fundamentally irrational and certainly reckless but it is not surprising. It is part of what the ecologist William Rees calls 'gross human ecological dysfunction'. By

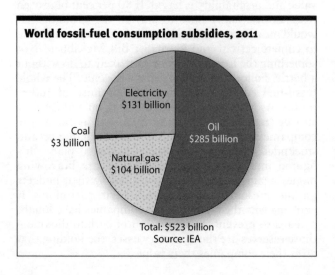

World fossil-fuel consumption subsidies, 2011

Electricity $131 billion

Coal $3 billion

Oil $285 billion

Natural gas $104 billion

Total: $523 billion
Source: IEA

that he means that humans see themselves as separate and apart from the natural world, that our economic systems have become myopic, self-interested and self-fulfilling. It's as if 'we float free from biophysical reality,' writes Rees, 'blind to the energy and material flows essential for human existence, to the state of vital natural capital stocks, and to the complex dynamics of the ecosystems that produce them.'[10]

Ecological footprints

Rees, along with colleague Mathis Wackernagel, pioneered the now familiar 'ecological footprint' concept, which attempts to put a number on the amount of ecological space occupied by people and by nations. It's a way of asking how much we are extracting from the planet in order to live the way we do. Conventional economics tends to see the environment as a subset of the economy. The footprint approach does the reverse, comparing humanity's ecological impact – resources consumed and waste produced – with the amount of productive land and water available to supply key ecosystem services.

It deals in averages, so the rich/poor divide is blurred. But the message is clear. Current estimates put the amount of land used to maintain the consumption of the average person in the West at around 6-10 hectares. However, the total available productive land in the world is about 1.8 hectares per person. The difference, they call 'appropriated carrying capacity' – which basically means the rich are living off the resources of the poor, either from elsewhere or from future generations.

Those of us in the rich world have a footprint way above the average. Canadians use about eight hectares, more than four times the world average. Americans use about 10 hectares, more than five times the average. The Netherlands consumes the output of a productive land mass four times its size while Japan's

$$\frac{6}{1.8} = 3.3 \qquad \frac{10}{1.8} = 5.5$$

eco-footprint is eight times greater than the country's domestic biocapacity. Most Northern countries and many urban regions in the South already consume more than their fair share; they depend on trade (using someone else's natural assets) or on depleting their own natural capital.

In 1961, human beings used about half the Earth's biocapacity. According to Rees and Wackernagel, the global footprint now exceeds global biocapacity by 20 per cent and that gap is growing yearly. The US alone, with 4.5 per cent of the world's population, sucks up 25 per cent of the earth's biocapacity. The average Indian has a global footprint of just 0.8 hectares while the average American has an ecological footprint of 9.7 hectares.

Such is our claim on the diminishing resources of the planet that Wackernagel estimates we will need the equivalent of two Earths by the late 2030s to keep up with our demands. Ecologists call this phenomenon 'overshoot'. It's a temporary state that becomes more untenable as stocks of renewable and non-renewable resources are depleted. 'Since the 1980s we've been drawing down the biosphere's principal rather than living off its annual interest. To support our consumption, we have been liquidating resource stocks and allowing carbon dioxide to accumulate in the atmosphere.'[11]

Faith in economic growth as the ultimate hope for human progress is widespread. A central tenet of economists on left and right has been that the 'carrying capacity' of the Earth is infinitely expandable. The underlying belief is that a combination of ingenuity and technology will eventually allow us all to live like middle-class Americans – if we can only ignore the naysayers and keep the economy growing. That road has now come to an end.

So Big Oil has a lot at stake – and a lot to answer for. The growth dynamic drives the companies forward. They spend billions every year scouring the globe in their search for more oil and gas; because this is what they do best and what they must do to meet their obligations to shareholders. Yet the 'inconvenient truth', to use the phrase of former US vice-president Al Gore, is that their normal business activities – providing hydrocarbons to fuel the global growth machine – now imperil both humankind and the biosphere itself.

Can we bring business on board before it's too late? Can we convince the fossil-fuel industry to act in the best interest of the planet? Of course, the answer is that we must. There is no other choice. But corporations and governments are having grave difficulty in conquering their addiction to oil, as we will see in the next chapter.

1 'Toronto's Future Weather & Climate Driver Study', Toronto Environment Office, 30 Oct 2012. 2 Tess Kalinowski, 'Toronto failing to act on alarming climate changes', *Toronto Star*, 11 Nov 2012. 3 'Turn Down the heat: Why a 4 degree centigrade warmer world must be avoided', World Bank, Nov 2012. 4 Janet Redman, 'Global Civil Society Wary of World Bank Role in New Funds', IPS, 5 Apr, 2011. 5 Justin Kilcullen, 'Climate change takes dark toll in death and destruction', *The Irish Times*, 20 Jun 2012. 6 Tom Kington, 'Italy floods prompt fears for future of farming', *The Guardian*, 13 Nov 2012. 7 Tim Jackson, *Prosperity without Growth*, Earthscan, 2009. 8 Bill McKibben, 'Global warming's terrifying new math', *Rolling Stone*, 19 Jul 2012. 9 Emily E Adams, 'The Energy Game is Rigged: Fossil Fuel Subsidies Topped $620 Billion in 2011', Earth Policy Institute, 27 Feb 2013, earth-policy. org 10 William E Rees, 'Towards a sustainable world', paper presented to the Institute for New Economic Thinking Annual Conference – Crisis and Renewal: International Political Economy at the Crossroads, Apr 2011. 11 'The Ecological Wealth of Nations', Global Footprint Network, 2010.

4 Peak oil and tar sands

Why oil is so powerful – and yet so exhaustible. Modern developments such as fracking and converting tar sands into oil are simply postponing the inevitable – and adding to climate chaos in the process.

'Petroleum Man will be virtually extinct this century, and Homo sapiens faces a major challenge in adapting to his loss.'

Colin J Campbell

Oil lies at the heart of the modern global economy. It is the lifeblood of growth; its influence so pervasive and so fundamental that we rarely think about how utterly dependent we are on the stuff. It is not just another commodity; it is 'the precondition of all commodities', an elemental energy source on which all human activity is premised. The more fossil fuels we burn – oil, coal or natural gas – the faster the economy grows. As Jeff Rubin, former chief economist at CIBC World Markets has written: 'On average over the last four decades, a 1-per-cent bump in world oil consumption has led to a 2-per-cent increase in global GDP. That means if GDP increased by 4 per cent a year – as it often did before the 2008 recession – oil consumption was increasing by 2 per cent a year.'[1]

Oil is an extraordinary feat of concentrated energy, the sun's raw power captured in organic matter over millions of years, then compressed and pressurized by geological forces for millennia. Scientists reckon that most of the petroleum we use was laid down now in two distinct periods of extreme warming, 90 and 150 million years ago, from vast blooms of algae in shallow tropical seas. Oil is an amazingly potent energy source: three large teaspoons of crude amazingly contain about the same amount of energy as eight hours of human manual labor. Oil-fueled inventions like the internal combustion engine have irrevocably changed the relationship between humans and the natural world. Two centuries ago our ancestors knew only animal power, wind power and water power. Time and culture moved at a slower pace. It wasn't until James Watt's invention of the steam engine in 1781, followed by steam-driven trains in the 1820s and 1830s, that human beings were able to move themselves and their possessions faster than a horse could run: which is of course why 'horsepower' became the metric for measuring the power of the internal combustion engine. The labor-saving energy of oil was revolutionary. One gallon of petrol/gasoline has the energy equivalent to 350-500 hours of human labor. Relentless speed-up became the new mantra. The outspoken British geologist, Colin J Campbell, hit the nail on the head when he said: 'It's as if each one of us had a team of slaves working for us for next to nothing.'[2]

Petroleum is the most important raw material on the planet and the central driver of economic growth. As with fresh air and clean water, it is assumed that we will never run out of the stuff. Yet the petroleum age has been a relatively short one. Barely 150 years have passed since the commercial oil era was launched almost simultaneously in the backwoods of Pennsylvania and near Baku, on the shores of the Caspian Sea. We may treat oil as if supplies are inexhaustible but like all other elements that we extract from the earth, 'black gold' is a finite resource. They're not making any more of it, at least not in any geological timeframe that we can wrap our heads around.

So when will we run out? And what happens before and after we get to that point?

These are questions to which few people – certainly not politicians, mainstream economists or business leaders – until very recently gave much thought. But, believe it or not, concerns about the end of oil have been in the air for more than half a century.

Peak oil and tar sands

Back in 1957, M King Hubbert, an irascible and brilliant oil geologist who worked for Shell Oil (and later the US Geological Survey) made what then seemed an outrageous claim. Hubbert showed that when oil is pumped from the ground the volume extracted follows a bell curve. Production starts slowly, and then climbs to a high point before beginning a slow decline. At maximum output, at the top of the curve, half the oil has been removed. That point is now referred to as 'Hubbert's Peak'. Having analyzed the history of oil exploration and discoveries till then the geologist predicted that oil production in the mainland United States would peak in 1970. This tipping point is sometimes referred to as 'the big rollover' – the point at which the demand for oil begins to exceed the rate at which new reserves are discovered.

'The consumption of energy from fossil fuels is thus seen to be a pip rising sharply from zero to a maximum, and almost as sharply declining,' Hubbert wrote, 'thus representing but a moment in human history.'[3] His peers dismissed him as a pessimist and a crank, but as the years passed Hubbert's calculations proved to be remarkably accurate. Apart from brief surges of supply from new wells in Alaska and the Gulf of Mexico and recent 'fracked' oil, data from the US Energy Information Administration shows that

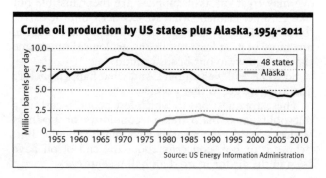

Crude oil production by US states plus Alaska, 1954-2011

Source: US Energy Information Administration

crude oil production peaked in the lower 48 states at 9.4 million barrels a day in 1970. Alaskan production bumped supply slightly but didn't stop the overall downward trend. And now Alaska is also in decline. In 2011, the largest US state pumped 0.6 million barrels a day, less than a third of its highest level in 1988. Production in the mainland US is now down to 3.4 million barrels a day (2012), roughly half the rate of 1970, and before the recent arrival of 'fracked' oil it was declining at about five per cent a year.[4]

Global peak oil

Hubbert applied the same analysis to global oil production, though here the data becomes murkier. He predicted that production would peak in 1995, which would be 'the deadline for alternative forms of energy that must replace petroleum in the sharp drop-off that follows'. That date has since slipped into history and billions of barrels of crude are still being pumped from the ground every year. In 2011, global oil consumption was around 87 million barrels a day with total reserves estimated at 1.3 billion barrels.[5] Global 'peak oil' has proved harder to predict. The main reason is that the key players – the big oil companies and the major producing countries in OPEC (the Organization of the Petroleum-Exporting Countries) – keep their cards close to their chests. Both have been known to manipulate and distort figures for market reasons. In OPEC, for example, the amount a country is allowed to export is linked to its 'proven reserves': the higher the reserves, the higher the export quota.

Saudi Arabia is the world's largest oil producer. Its vast Ghawar field produces half the country's daily output and more than five per cent of world output. Over its 60-year life it has produced an ocean of oil. But the country releases almost no public information about its output. And the data it does release is highly suspect. It's clear that no new oil has been discovered in Saudi Arabia in half a century. Yet its reserves have remained constant at 260 billion barrels – even though it has pumped out more than 100 billion barrels over the same period.[6] So estimates of production and reserves tend to be 'fluid'. The upshot is that it is almost impossible to predict when the global supply peak will arrive; only that accelerating demand will inevitably crash into the brick wall of finite reserves. Nonetheless, on a country-by-country basis the endgame is clearly in sight. The combination of dwindling supply coupled with fewer new discoveries and diminishing overall supply is taking hold. Of the more than 50 petro-leum-exporting nations in the world, 40 are past peak production. Australia hit peak oil in 2000 and now imports 40 per cent of its needs. The UK's North Sea oil peaked in 1999 even though the UK and Scottish governments estimate that 24 billion barrels of oil remain to be exploited over the next four decades. Conventional oil production in Canada peaked in 1973 though production of synthetic crude from the country's enormous tar-sands deposits continues to expand.

British geologist Colin J Campbell, mentioned above, notes that the peak of oil discovery was in the 1960s and that by 1981 the world was already using more than was being found in new fields. And, he says, the gap between discovery and production has widened since.

Here's an excerpt from Campbell's 'Understanding Peak Oil', from the website of the Association for the Study of Peak Oil (ASPO), an organization he founded in 2001. ASPO is one of the leading sources of clear, unfiltered data on the whole peak oil debate.

> Many countries, including some important producers, have already passed their peak, suggesting that the world peak of production is now imminent. Were valid data available in the public domain, it would be a simple matter to determine both the date of peak and the rate of

subsequent decline, but as it is, we find a maze of conflicting information, ambiguous definitions and lax reporting procedures...

Despite the uncertainties of detail, it is now evident that the world faces the dawn of the second half of the Age of Oil, when this critical commodity, which plays such a fundamental part in the modern economy, heads into decline due to natural depletion.

A debate rages over the precise date of the peak, but rather misses the point, when what matters – and matters greatly – is the vision of the long remorseless decline that comes into sight on the other side of it. The transition to decline threatens to be a time of great international tension.[7]

Recent events indicate that the 'long remorseless decline' has arrived. The relationship between supply and demand is evident: if exports are cut, or delivery lines are pinched by war or weather, supplies dwindle and prices surge. When oil is cheap the global economic system hums along. When it's expensive the tune changes and things get nasty. We have seen the results as recently as 2008 when the price of crude shot up to $147 per barrel and the global economy nose-dived into a steep recession from which it has still not recovered. This price increase was like adding a $3-trillion surcharge to the global energy bill, a move that effectively sucked demand from every other market sector and contributed to the collapse of the global banking system. These oil price shocks have occurred repeatedly since the early 1970s, always with earth-shaking consequences.

Forty years ago, prompted by Western support for Israel during the Yom Kippur War, OPEC quadrupled the price of oil from $4 to $16 a barrel. The move had been a long time coming. Two years previously the US had single-handedly sabotaged the post-war Bretton

Woods monetary regime by suddenly declaring that the US would no longer peg the dollar to gold. (The reasons were complex but vast debts from paying for the Vietnam War were central.) With the gold standard in tatters and the dollar hugely devalued, Washington was effectively able to make the rest of the world pay for the war. OPEC was understandably desperate to regain the diminished value of its dollar-dominated oil exports.

Oil shocks

'Oil as a weapon' became the catch-phrase. The ripples were felt around the globe. Long lines of anxious drivers queued outside petrol/gas stations across Europe and North America. The US even lowered its highway speed limit to 55 miles per hour to save on oil imports. The global economy ground to a halt as inflation triggered by high petroleum prices seeped through the system. The knock-on effects were dramatic. Flush with millions of dollars, OPEC nations channeled bucketloads of cash back into the US and European banking systems, in what came to be known as 'petro-dollar recycling'. Much of that easy money was then loaned back to poor countries, supposedly to pay for oil imports. In fact most of it was 'recycled' into the pockets of corrupt dictators (Ferdinand Marcos in the Philippines and Mobutu Sese Seko in the Democratic Republic of the Congo were two of the most reviled) or was used to finance ludicrous mega-projects – in the process crippling those struggling developing nations with massive debt loads. Within a year, GDP in the US had shrunk by nearly three per cent and the global economy had tipped into 'stagflation' – an unprecedented combination of negative growth and galloping inflation.

The peak-oil crunch means disruptions caused by costly crude will become commonplace and that the global economy will continue to be whipsawed by the vagaries of supply. As oil analyst David Greely, of the investment bank Goldman Sachs, said recently: 'It is only a matter of time before inventories and OPEC spare capacity become effectively exhausted, requiring higher oil prices to restrain demand.'[8]

The crippling recession we have experienced since 2008 is the face of the future, even as oil companies continue to prod and bore the earth in an attempt to expand reserves. But the oil will no longer be cheap. There are no more Saudi Arabias waiting in the wings. The easily accessible, high-grade stuff is now gone. Instead, companies have set their sights on more expensive, energy-intensive, technically challenging and environmentally dangerous exploration.

They're opening offshore wells in the deep waters of the world's oceans. They're scrambling to lay claim to an estimated 90 billion barrels of oil in the high Arctic. They're ravaging irreplaceable tropical rainforests in Asia and Latin America. And they're 'fracking' oil shales to force long-trapped pockets of oil and gas to the surface in the US and Canada. Indeed, hydraulic fracturing, or 'fracking', is on a roll – despite widespread worry about environmental impacts, including its effect on the water table.

Due to new supplies of fracked gas, the US is now able to meet 90 per cent of its needs. Oil insiders predict that North Dakota's Bakken field, plus other 'plays' in Texas and Pennsylvania, may soon bump US shale-oil output to five million barrels a day. The Paris-based International Energy Agency forecasts that the US will be producing a total of 11.1 million barrels a day by 2020, up from 8.1 million barrels in 2011. Yet even fracked oil is costly compared to conventional crude. When world oil prices dipped in the summer of 2012, shale-oil workers in North Dakota were given extended holidays. 'Supposedly cheap shale turned out to be rather expensive shale in that, as soon as Brent [a standard benchmark price for sweet, light crude] fell to $90 per barrel, a large proportion of US shale oil in key regions seemed to lose all its rent,' noted Paul Horsnell from Barclays Capital.[8]

But perhaps the largest amounts of hype and cash are being poured into the bitumen-soaked tar sands in Canada's western province of Alberta. Almost every major oil company – including Total SA, ExxonMobil, Shell, BP and Chevron – owns a chunk of the tar sands. State-owned companies, especially from China, are also active. Sinopec, for example, owns part of Syncrude Canada and all of Daylight Energy. And in December 2012 the China National Offshore Oil Corporation (CNOOC) snapped up Calgary-based oil and gas company Nexen in a contentious $15.1-billion deal.

Canada's tar sands

Big Oil has ploughed more than $200 billion so far into the tar sands and Alberta is projecting an additional $218 billion in investment over the next 25 years, which could boost output to more than three million barrels a day. Nearly 1.5 million hectares of northern boreal forest have been razed, with devastating consequences for the ecology of the region as well as for the Cree and Chipewyan people whose ancestral lands are being pillaged. Cancer rates are skyrocketing in native communities like Fort Chipewyan, whose water supply from the Athabasca River watershed is used to process the bitumen. First Nations communities in the area have called for a moratorium on future oil-sands development. And the Athabasca Chipewyan First Nation has launched a constitutional challenge to Shell Canada's attempt to expand its Jackpine mine. Shell wants to pump another 18 million cubic meters of water a year from the Athabasca River to operate the mine.[9]

The tar-sands development is so enormous that it defies imagination. The scar on the land from the non-stop excavation and the 'tailing ponds' (actually enormous lakes that hold the toxic wastes from mining) can be seen in photographs from orbiting satellites. The 'ponds', which cover more than 140 square kilometers along the Athabasca River, contain a carcinogenic brew of industrial chemicals including cyanide, ammonia, mercury, arsenic, naphthenic acids and polycyclic aromatic hydrocarbons. In total, more than 75 toxic compounds have been found.

Synthetic crude from Alberta now makes up a quarter of Canada's exports and the impact of this oil money on the national economy and political culture has been enormous. In the words of one critic, Canada has become a 'dysfunctional petro state' where the interests of Big Oil and the interests of the government have merged to trample the public interest.

As Stanford political scientist Terry Lynn Karl cautions in her book, *The Paradox of Plenty: Oil Booms and Petro States*: 'Oil revenues are the catalyst for a chronic tendency of the state to become overextended, over-centralized and captured by special interests.'

This single-minded focus on tar-sands oil has destabilized the rest of the economy, turning the Canadian dollar into an inflated 'petro currency', which has in turn hobbled the domestic manufacturing industry. A strong dollar has priced Canadian goods out of international markets while commodity exports have increased. From 2004 to 2010, more than 550,000 jobs were lost in manufacturing: experts say more than half of these losses were due to Canada's overpriced currency. Even so, this shift has had little impact on a federal government dazzled by oil revenues.

Carbon disaster

The Canadian state has become so addicted to oil money that concern about CO_2 emissions has disappeared from government policy. Once considered a sensible middle-power, the country has morphed into an intolerant climate skeptic. At the 2010 Copenhagen climate talks, the global activist group Avaaz awarded its 'Fossil of the Year' award to Canada. Avaaz spokes-person Ben Wikler commented: 'Canada's performance here in Copenhagen builds on two years of delay, obstruction and total inaction. This government thinks there's a choice between environment and economy and for them, tar sands beats climate every time. Canada's emissions are headed nowhere but up.'[9]

At the moment carbon emissions from the tar sands are approaching 50 million tonnes a year. But they're projected to double by 2020, at which point Alberta will be pumping more carbon into the atmosphere than European countries like Austria, Belgium, Denmark, Greece, Hungary and Ireland.[10]

The European Commission (EU) says that bitumen production has a carbon footprint 22 per cent higher than conventional oil. The EU has yet to brand synthetic crude a danger to the global climate – only because of intense lobbying from Ottawa. The Canadian government worries that such a ban would set a global precedent limiting future oil-sands growth and has reportedly threatened a trade war with Europe if the 'dirty oil' classification were to be passed.

Concern over growing foreign opposition to tar-sands exports prompted the Canadian government to spend $16.5 million on 'responsible resource development' print, TV and online ads in 2013. The oil companies are also anxious that anti-tar sands campaigns are gaining traction and are spending millions on slick, feel-good ads to counter the message that oil spills and greenhouse-gas emissions are a worry. In an escalating public-relations battle, the Canadian Association of Petroleum Producers reports that it has spent millions on ads every year since 2010.[11]

What is not up for debate, at least not in saner quarters of the scientific community, is what all that CO_2 is doing to the planet. The mechanics of 'global warming', increasing temperatures via the 'greenhouse effect', are fairly simple. Greenhouse gases (mainly carbon dioxide, which makes up 77 per cent of global emissions, but also carbon monoxide, methane, nitrous oxide, carbon tetrafluoride) hold the sun's energy, preventing it from bouncing back into the atmosphere. The gases act like a cozy blanket, trapping heat from infrared radiation, thus keeping the planet warm. Without this natural greenhouse effect we'd be much colder and the Earth would be a very miserable place indeed.

It is reckoned that greenhouse gases warm the planet by about 30 degrees Celsius compared to what it would be otherwise. The problem is that humans have turned up the thermostat by burning billions of tonnes of coal, gas and oil, inflating the volume of greenhouse gases far beyond the natural levels of 200-300 parts per million (ppm). Since the industrial revolution, 250 years ago, we have released close to 1,800 gigatonnes (1 gigatonne = 1 billion tonnes) of CO_2 into the atmosphere and this has made our cozy blanket more like an overheated duvet. In May 2013 the concentration of CO_2 at the Mauna Loa monitoring station in Hawaii passed 400 ppm, a level not seen on Earth since the Pliocene Era three million years ago. The geological record shows that sea levels were 60-80 feet higher then and summer temperatures in the Arctic 10 degrees warmer.[12] Despite lofty pledges to reduce carbon emissions, the world produces 48 per cent more CO_2 now than it did in 1992 when the first Rio summit on climate change took place. And China, the world's most populous nation, has now surpassed the US as the world's biggest CO_2 emitter, releasing 8.3 gigatonnes in 2010 and accounting for over 25 per cent of the global total.

According to the UN's blue-ribbon Intergovernmental Panel on Climate Change, our profligate use of fossil fuels is paving the way to climate chaos. This select group of 2,500 of the world's top climate scientists paints a disturbing picture of what our collective future might hold if we continue to place our faith in carbon-based economic growth: extreme weather, rising sea levels, melting glaciers, spreading disease, climate refugees, oil wars.

But if we are to do something about this we will also need to understand how debt, the financial market and the nature of capitalism itself are all part of the problem.

1 Jeff Rubin, *The end of growth: But is that all bad?* Random House, 2012. **2** Cited in Thomas Homer-Dixon, *The upside of down*, Knopf, 2006. **3** Pat Murphy, *Plan C: Community Survival Strategies for Peak Oil and Climate Change*, New Society, 2008. **4**, **5** www.eia.gov **6** *Growth isn't possible*, New Economics Foundation, 2010. **7** www.peakoil.net/about-peak-oil **8** Ambrose Evans-Pritchard, 'Peak cheap oil is an incontrovertible fact', *The Telegraph*, 26 Aug 2012. **9** www.fossil-of-the-day.org **10** 'Greenhouse gas emission trends and projections in Europe 2011', European Environment Agency, Oct 2011. **11** Kelly Cryderman, 'Big oil's push to move the mushy middle', *Globe and Mail*, 11 Jun 2013. **12** Justin Gillis, 'Heat-trapping gas passes milestone, raising fears', *New York Times*, 10 May 2013.

5 Profits, debt and the growth imperative

Almost all countries are driving in a capitalist vehicle that only functions when there is economic growth. Extraordinary measures are sometimes needed to keep the whole show on the road, including making war and depending on debt. But neoliberal commitments to market freedom led inexorably to the 2008 crash – and to profound questions about this whole model.

'There is either a crisis or a return to the norm of stagnation... In Europe and the US, it's low growth and stagnation and a very sharp income differentiation, a shift – a striking shift – from production to financialization...'

Noam Chomsky

We live in a world that is addicted to growth. Apart from isolated oddities like North Korea and Cuba there are few places where some form of growth-dependent capitalism does not reign supreme. The model may vary in small ways from country to country but the make is the same. There are more similarities than differences. Western nations like France, Britain, Germany, Australia and the US preach the sanctity of open markets and the free flow of capital – although some states are more 'interventionist' than others.

The emerging BRIC countries – Brazil, Russia, India and China – each have a slightly different kind of economic model. Russia operates a 'wild west' capitalism where powerful oligarchs linked to the Kremlin control resource extraction industries and reap the benefits. India, too, has plumped for globalized markets, opening its borders to foreign corporations and giving its own hyper-active entrepreneurs *carte blanche* to do the same, modernizing the country but also widening the rich/poor gap. Brazil has a social conscience, and has been tackling poverty in a serious way over the past decade with the aid of its *bolsa familia*, a monthly cash transfer to the poor. More than 36 million have been helped by the program since 2003. But it is also one of the most unequal countries in the world. It has giant corporations (Brazil's Vale is the world's second largest mining company, with reported profits of $22 billion in 2011), a robust manufacturing sector, an entrenched land-owning élite and a booming trade in agricultural exports.

Much has been written about the extraordinary growth of the Chinese economy since Deng Xiaoping decided to 'let some people get rich first', opening up to private business in 1979. In 1992 China officially became a 'socialist market economy'. During the next decade most state-owned enterprises were privatized and tens of millions of state workers were laid off. China is urbanizing at lightning speed. A billion people will move from the countryside into cities by 2025, the largest migration in human history, and there are already more than 250 million migrant workers. China is now a full-throttle capitalist nation, the sparkplug of the global system. The ruling Communist Party runs a tight, authoritarian ship. But it is not a democracy. Corruption is rampant, the environment is under assault and the gap between rich and poor, one of the largest in the world, is growing.

So capitalism wears different masks. It's an adaptable system with a chameleon-like ability to adapt to different political configurations. But the common denominator is growth: all these countries depend on an expanding economy to legitimize their power and to mask the inequalities generated by the system itself. The surprising thing is how tough it is to keep things moving and how prone the system is to breakdown. Crises appear with regularity. Recession, inflation, stagnation, 'market corrections' and the gyrations of the 'business cycle' are a familiar part of the boom-and-bust we've come to expect. But if crises and instability are part of the package then growth is the default solution. It's braided into the DNA of capitalism, a structural necessity; without it, the system would fragment and soon collapse.

There is no argument with the claim that the market system has propelled the world into an era of unparalleled prosperity and material well-being. On average, in Western countries we live longer, healthier, freer, more mobile and materially richer lives than our parents and our grandparents. In what used to be called the 'Third World' lives have improved dramatically too. In 1981, 84 per cent of China's people lived in extreme poverty. By 2005 that had fallen to 16 per cent – a booming economy lifted more than 500 million Chinese out of poverty in less than 25 years. Meanwhile in Vietnam the extreme poverty rate dropped by 42 per cent between 1993 and 2006.

And in Brazil, according to the World Bank, the number of people living in poverty fell from 21 per cent of the population in 2003 to 11 per cent in 2009. Extreme poverty (people living on less than $1.25 per day) also dropped from 10 per cent in 2004 to 2.2 per cent in 2009.[1]

So economic growth in poor countries can make a real difference in people's lives. But it has far from an unblemished record. The gale of 'creative destruction', the motive force of capitalism described by Austrian economist Joseph Schumpeter, also brings with it environmental devastation, social dislocation and corrosive inequality. A single-minded fixation on growth also undercuts democracy. When growth is seen as the only way forward, it's no surprise that powerful forces who know best how to work the system – bankers, financiers and corporate leaders – have the loudest voices and can bend things to their advantage.

Contradictions in capitalism

Our global economy seems to need growth to survive. The two are like conjoined twins. They can't be separated without fatal consequences for both. Why is that the case?

Karl Marx, one of the great economic thinkers of the 19th century, was a perceptive critic of capitalism. His reputation was tarnished by totalitarian regimes in the former Soviet Union and elsewhere that called themselves 'marxist' – though it is likely that the luxuriantly bearded philosopher would have been repelled by the association. But lately, as the global slowdown grinds on, the core of his analysis has been dusted off and revalidated. Even mainstream economists like Nouriel Roubini suggest that Marx was on to something. Roubini, a former Yale professor and White House advisor, told the *Wall Street Journal*: 'Karl Marx had it right. At some point capitalism can destroy itself because you cannot continue shifting income from labor to capital without having excess capacity and a lack of aggregate demand... my labor costs are somebody else's labor income and consumption. That's why it's a self-destructive process.'[2]

Writing amidst the tumult and social upheaval of the industrial revolution, Marx saw the main force driving the system as the endless accumulation of capital. 'Accumulate, accumulate, that is Moses and the Prophets,' he wrote in Volume 1 of his magnum opus, *Capital*. By that, Marx meant that profit, not production, was the overriding preoccupation of the owners of capital.

Why is profit so central? In most nation-states, companies are legally bound to maximize returns to shareholders – and even leaving aside the legal requirement, doing otherwise would risk investors pulling out their money and investing it elsewhere. Profits, investor value and growth are intimately linked. Without steady growth, share value would fall, driving away investors, sending the whole business into a downward spiral. Instead, companies must constantly look for bigger profits to reward investors. The only way to do this is by operating more efficiently: to lower the cost per unit of output and thereby gain the upper hand on competitors by lowering prices. You can also cut costs by pressuring suppliers to lower the price of inputs. And some large, powerful businesses with a dominant market share can do this. The US-based retail giant Walmart, one of the world's richest companies, is a case in point. But a more effective strategy is to replace human labor with up-to-date, labor-saving technology.

This is what Nouriel Roubini was pointing out. In the short term, a business may lower costs by substituting technology for labor, thereby increasing both output and profits. But this has a couple of knock-on effects. The first is that those workers you've laid off collectively have less money to spend on the things you're producing. It's a zero sum game: my spending is your income and vice versa. Second, all that increased production tends to lead to over-supply, which inevitably depresses both price and profit.

This falling rate of profit is a serious problem. But it's not insurmountable if you can 'grow' your way out of the dilemma. Economic expansion – growth – is the safety valve. The theory is that when businesses expand they can re-employ some of those workers pushed aside by technology. With wages in hand, those workers regain confidence and begin to venture into the marketplace again. Companies thus increase their sales and profits, at least until the same logic reasserts itself and the whole process starts again.

That's why capitalism is so dynamic. Standing still is not an option. If you want to survive as a business you cannot rest on your laurels. If you do, your competitors will be snapping at your heels. It's grow or die: there is no other choice under the current set-up.

Unless you keep pace, you'll be driven out of business or swallowed by a competitor. Yet the irony is that while capitalism is utterly dependent on growth for its survival it also has a built-in tendency to slow growth, or stagnate. The system is a victim of its own success. Competition for bigger markets and more sales both slices profit margins and paves the way to monopoly as successful corporations swallow their less successful competitors. This jockeying for position via mergers and acquisitions is 'unproductive' in the real sense that investment is not being used to expand capacity or produce more 'stuff'. Nonetheless, this competitive jousting occupies a huge amount of corporate brainpower. Essentially it's a way of cutting costs by consolidating production, closing factories and laying off workers. In the short run it boosts the bottom line but in the long run it's self-defeating since it inevitably reduces aggregate demand.

Henry Ford, the notoriously antisemitic father of the automobile assembly line, realized nearly a century ago that a company can run into problems when wages are depressed and workers replaced with machines. After a while you're producing millions of cars but you have few people who can buy them. It's the classic dilemma of too many goods and too few buyers. That's exactly the situation today. We have the capacity to produce far more 'stuff' than we need or can be sold. There is a global over-capacity in everything from shoes and steel to clothing and electronic goods. China is the world's number one producer of consumer goods. Yet the country used just 60 per cent of its manufacturing capacity in 2011, according to the International Monetary Fund (IMF). Eliminating excess capacity, said the IMF, won't be achieved without 'structural reforms' to move the economy 'away from investment and toward consumption' which would translate into 'slower but higher-quality growth over the medium term'. China's 40-per-cent excess capacity compares to

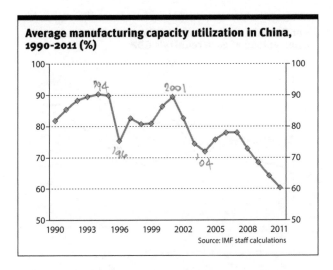

Average manufacturing capacity utilization in China, 1990-2011 (%)

Source: IMF staff calculations

about 20 per cent for the US, Canada, Germany and other OECD nations. Why would investors want to sink their funds into new plants and equipment when existing factories are not running at full speed?

So businesses are left sitting on profits, reluctant to invest when capacity is already vastly underutilized. In recent years corporations have been hauled over the coals for squirreling away huge chunks of cash instead of plowing it back into useful investment. The Internal Revenue Service in Washington says US companies worldwide in 2009 had stockpiled $4.8 trillion in liquid assets. According to the *Wall Street Journal* (WSJ), corporations in the US, the euro zone, the UK and Japan held some $7.75 trillion in cash in 2012. Simon Tilford, chief economist at the Centre for European Reform in London, told the WSJ that the ratio of investment to gross domestic product in Europe is at a 60-year low while corporate cash holdings hit $2.64 trillion across the euro zone and $1.19 trillion in the UK.[3] Meanwhile, ex-Bank of Canada governor

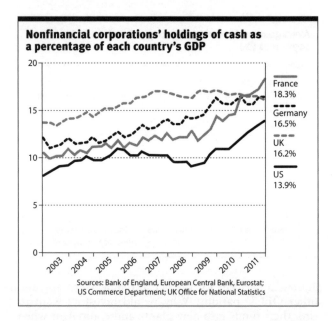

Nonfinancial corporations' holdings of cash as a percentage of each country's GDP

France 18.3%
Germany 16.5%
UK 16.2%
US 13.9%

Sources: Bank of England, European Central Bank, Eurostat; US Commerce Department; UK Office for National Statistics

Mark Carney (now piloting the Bank of England) criticized Canadian corporations in August 2012 for hoarding almost $600 billion of unused cash instead of circulating it back into the economy. 'This is dead money,' Carney complained. 'If companies can't figure out what to do with it, then they should give it to shareholders and they'll figure it out.'

How war can help...

Let's recap the main points. As industries consolidate to cut losses, factories are closed but output remains the same or increases. This produces a falling rate of profit, which in turn drives industry to look for further efficiencies. One tack is to continue to cut labor costs – which may help the bottom line initially but over time actually dampens global demand as jobless workers rein in their spending. The upshot, as Mark Carney pointed out, is that investors either sit on their cash or look for *other* ways to grow and make a profit.

So what happens when investment returns are anemic in the goods-producing economy? What are some of those other ways that capital can seek growth and profits?

Sometimes revolutionary inventions can expand investment opportunities and open up a whole new wave of production. The steam engine and railways provided a route out of stagnation in the 19th century. Air transport and automobiles did the same thing in the early and mid-20th century. Recently, computers and digital technology have provided an opportunity for accelerating the growth cycle. But even radically new investment ideas soon lose their luster as the cycle gradually asserts itself: competition → falling rates of profit → excess capacity → stagnation.

When there have not been obvious new ways of turning a profit, corporations have looked to friends in high places for help. A sure-fire way of doing this has been to convince governments to devote large chunks of their budget to buying armaments and waging war. Military spending is a kind of perverted 'Keynesianism'. Public funds are diverted to boost unproductive and inflationary industries. People are employed, resources are used, profits are made and growth is stimulated. But to what end? Dollar for dollar, investments in clean energy, healthcare and education provide a much better chance of good jobs than the same amount of spending on the military. The US spent $188 billion waging wars in Afghanistan and Iraq in 2008 according to the Congressional Research Service. That same year the total US military budget was $624 billion – eight times the amount spent on education.

The Stockholm International Peace Research Institute (SIPRI), estimates that total world military spending in 2011 reached $1.74 trillion, exceeding what was spent at the height of the 'Cold War'. Indeed, *The*

Top ten defense budgets (2011)

Rank	Country	Spending ($ billion)	World Share (%)	% of GDP, 2011
1	United States	711.0	41.0	4.7
2	China	143.0	8.2	2.0
3	Russia	71.9	4.1	3.9
4	United Kingdom	62.7	3.6	2.6
5	France	62.5	3.6	2.3
6	Japan	59.3	3.4	1.0
7	India	48.9	2.8	2.5
8	Saudi Arabia	48.5	2.8	8.7
9	Germany	46.7	2.7	1.3
10	Brazil	35.4	2.0	1.5
	World Total	**1735**	**74.3**	**2.5**

Source: SIPRI

Economist found that in 2010 'American defense spending exceeded the average spent during the Cold War years by 50 per cent (adjusted for inflation), while in the past 10 years it has grown by 67 per cent in real terms'.[4]

Waging war and buying armaments is one way to keep growth ticking. But even so it has not been enough to prevent the system drifting into stagnation. What else is left?

...and so can debt

Since the early 1980s, debt and financial speculation have been even more important than military spending in providing profitable outlets for investors. In simple terms, the payment of interest on debt is similar to the expectation of profits on investment. As the expectation of profit drives growth so does the demand for interest. Debt thus becomes a means and a motive for economic expansion.

Here's how it works. Money is a means of exchange; it has no use value in itself. Ideally, there should be a close correlation between the 'real' physical economy and the money in circulation that represents a claim on those assets. But this is not how our financial system works. Why? Well, because money is in essence created out of thin air. Banks legally lend out a lot more money than they have on deposit, based on the assumption that all customers will not want their money back at the same time. (Though, in unusual circumstances, this does happen. In September 2007, at the start of the great financial meltdown, one of Britain's biggest mortgage lenders, Northern Rock, was faced with long queues of customers attempting to withdraw deposits as news of the bank's imminent collapse spread.) In most Western countries banks are obliged to hold on to around 8 per cent of deposited funds. The rest can be loaned – again and again. Banks and other financial institutions thus create money with a few computer key strokes just by lending it. The system is called 'fractional reserve banking'.

Loans, of course, come with interest attached. The difference between what a bank pays to depositors and what it collects on loans is one way banks make money. When an interest-bearing loan is repaid, the principal plus the interest become the assets for more loans, feeding the cycle. This compounding continues exponentially so that there is always more debt than there is money.

As long as the economy is growing this usually isn't a problem. Tomorrow's expansion provides the collateral for today's debt. New money (and new debt) is constantly created so existing debt can be repaid. A small number of loans slip into default but those losses are budgeted into overall profit targets. It's a delicate balance, however.

At the moment the world is swimming in debt. Levels of corporate debt and national (sovereign) debt are at an all-time high. In fact the situation has worsened substantially since the 2007/08 financial crash. Credit cards are maxed out and households are strained to the breaking point. Countries like Greece, Spain and Italy face massive budget deficits and crushing debt burdens. Across the Global South, debt repayment diverts millions from more pressing needs such as healthcare and education. When the financial crisis struck in 2008, the Jubilee Debt Campaign estimated the total debt for the 128 poorest countries at nearly $4 trillion, with debt service for those same countries totaling $602 billion. The total debt load has increased significantly since then as many governments have introduced 'fiscal stimulus packages' to combat the collapse. The McKinsey Global Institute (MGI) says that growth after the 2008 collapse has been buoyed by a $4.4 trillion increase in sovereign debt with the ratio of global debt to GDP increasing from 218 per cent in 2000 to 266 per cent in 2010. In an analysis of more than 75 countries, MGI found that 'the growth of government debt', especially in China, accounted for the majority of the increase in credit globally. We're often told that China's booming economy is critical to global prosperity but apparently even there debt is crucial.[5]

Keynesian remedies

As the economy grows or retracts, the repercussions are felt from top to bottom. In the upswing, jobs are created, production expands, more consumer goods are churned out and, ideally, incomes rise as unemployment falls. Growth means that governments can then raise additional taxes from businesses and consumers so that more public funds are available for things like schools, hospitals, roads, sewers and power grids. But when growth slows, good lending opportunities become scarce. Indebtedness rises faster than income, debt service becomes more difficult, bankruptcies and layoffs increase. As US critics Fred Magdoff and John Bellamy Foster explain:

'No-growth capitalism is an oxymoron: when growth ceases, the system is in a state of crisis.' The upshot is that the natural environment on which human life and the human economy depend is sidelined – 'not as a place with inherent boundaries within which human beings must live together with earth's other species, but as a realm to be exploited in a process of growing economic expansion.'[6]

Central banks, following the sage advice of John Maynard Keynes, used to have a way of countering the downside of the cycle. When growth slowed, they would buy government bonds on the open market, which would in turn drive down the interest rate of the bonds. The logic was that investors would soon abandon low-yielding bonds and look for alternative investments, thus stimulating growth. But in today's slow-growth environment investors aren't tempted. And with interest rates near zero there's no room to lower rates further to offer stimulus. Instead, governments resort to a monetary policy which economists call 'quantitative easing'. Essentially this means pumping more 'liquidity' into the system. The hope is that increasing the money supply will lead to more lending and borrowing by investors and consumers which will increase demand and, eventually, create more jobs. Former World Bank Chief Economist Joseph Stiglitz acknowledges that quantitative easing can produce a short-term blip. But he stresses that in countries like Spain, 'where so much money has fled the banking system… just adding liquidity, while continuing current austerity policies' will not be enough to spark renewed growth.[7]

This notion that growth-based prosperity tomorrow depends on investment today is fundamental to the structure of the economy. This conviction governs our own lives as much as it does the larger economy and mediates our relationship with the economic structures that surround us. Planning for retirement now means maximizing savings and the way to do that is to search for the best return on investment: savings accounts or bonds that pay the highest interest rates, stocks whose value will grow fastest. The markets feed on growth and we have little choice but to plan our own personal financial needs, as governments and companies plan their budgets, based on projections of future income. The growth addiction, like debt, is deeply rooted.

As we've seen, debt has exploded over the last 30 years in an era of open capital markets. Indeed, much of the economic growth that we've experienced during that time has been driven by debt. This dependency is part and parcel of a deliberate move to open the global economy to finance capital. Things began to shift around 1980 when free-market fundamentalists gained the upper hand, deriding the interventionist policies of post-World War Two Keynesianism. These 'neoliberals' believed government was the problem and that the market should be given free rein to perform its magic. The theory was that free trade and the wholesale removal of barriers to the flow of capital would boost growth. Markets, they argued, should be left alone to regulate themselves. This was not the consensus of those who wrote the rules for running the post-War economy at Bretton Woods, New Hampshire, in the summer of 1944. Their concern was that huge flows of unregulated capital would put too much power into the hands of wealthy investors and restrict the political power of countries to shape their own economic destiny. Keynes, the British delegate to the Bretton Woods Conference, was especially wary of fickle, profit-hungry investors and rampant speculation, which he saw as a clear threat to global economic stability.

In his 1936 tome, *The General Theory of Employment, Interest and Money*, Keynes wrote: 'Speculators may do no harm as bubbles on a steady stream of enterprise. But the position is serious when enterprise becomes the bubble on a whirlpool of speculation. When the capital development of a country becomes a by-product of the activities of a casino, the job is likely to be ill-done.'[8]

The birth of neoliberalism

Keynes's fears of a 'casino economy' were well founded. In the mid-1980s there was a systematic effort by governments in the UK and the US to deregulate their finance and banking industries, making it easier for investors to repatriate profits and to shift capital at a moment's notice. Margaret Thatcher's Conservative government in Britain was first off the mark when it launched what became known as the 'Big Bang' in London's financial markets in October 1986. De-regulation opened the door to free-wheeling trading in exotic financial products with little government oversight.

This neoliberal model soon became the flavor of the day. Most Western countries and later many developing countries – pressured by the World Bank and the IMF – followed suit. Like cascading dominoes, trade and investment barriers fell as economic globalization took hold. Investment bankers, corporate CEOs, bond traders and money managers were looking for more lucrative ways to invest their surplus capital than merely producing commodities. International finance seemed the obvious answer. Gambling in money markets was less work than investing to build a business from scratch. Soon trillions of dollars were flowing through global currency markets. The UN Conference on Trade and Development (UNCTAD) now puts the figure at more than $4 trillion – every day! Only a tiny sliver of this money is connected to the production of real goods and services: UNCTAD estimates just one per cent of foreign exchange trading is related to merchandise trade. Mostly, it is just money chasing money in an endless swirl of unproductive, frenzied speculation.

Boosters of financial deregulation argue that economic growth and prosperity inevitably follow open capital markets. Yet there is little proof to support this claim at the macro level. Over the past few decades the International Labour Organization (ILO) has documented a steady shift in the split of global income from wages to profits, making it more difficult for ordinary working people to make ends meet in the current crisis. This is occurring across the industrialized world, though it is less pronounced in the fast-growing countries of the Global South. The ILO's *Global Wage Report 2012/13* found labor's share of total income in 16 developed economies fell from 75 per cent in the mid-1970s to 65 per cent by 2007, just before the current economic crisis.[9] It edged up again in 2008 and 2009 but only because national income itself shrank.

Equally concerning is the growing gap between productivity growth and wage growth. Wages are not rising along with productivity. Instead the gains are

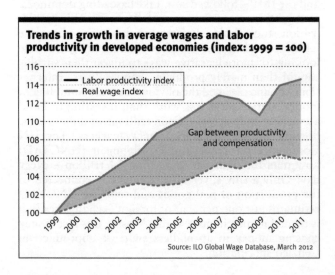

Trends in growth in average wages and labor productivity in developed economies (index: 1999 = 100)

- Labor productivity index
- Real wage index

Gap between productivity and compensation

Source: ILO Global Wage Database, March 2012

going into the pockets of employers and investors. The ILO says average labor productivity in developed economies increased more than twice as much as average wages from 1999 to 2011. For example, in the US, labor productivity has increased by about 85 per cent since 1980, while pay has increased by only 35 per cent. In Germany, productivity ballooned by 25 per cent over the past two decades but real monthly wages remained flat. As a result says the ILO, there has been a global shift in the distribution of national income – labor's share has decreased while capital's share has increased in a majority of countries. Even in China, where wages roughly tripled over the last decade, things are not as they seem. Since GDP increased faster than wages, labor's proportional share of total income actually dropped. The ILO points to labor-replacing technology and the weakening of the trade union movement as two causes of this shift. But the UN agency also notes that 'financial globalization may have played a bigger role than previously thought'.

Bigger indeed: finance capital has now become so dominant in the global economy that it has flipped the traditional capitalist model on its head. As the influential Marxist economist Paul Sweezy wrote back in 1994: 'The old structure of the economy, consisting of a production system served by a modest financial adjunct, had given way to a new structure in which a greatly expanded financial sector had achieved a high degree of independence and sat on top of the underlying production system.'[10] In plain language, debt-driven 'financialization' has been the escape hatch from endemic stagnation and the route back to growth. But what kind of growth and at what cost?

The 2008 crash
We only need to examine the years since the 2008 crash to see the results of a system dependent on what Keynes called 'a whirlpool of speculation'. By now the

details of what has become known as the 'sub-prime mortgage crisis' are well known. A combination of greed and avid speculation by banks, mortgage companies and investment firms led to a colossal housing bubble in the US and Europe, especially in the UK. House prices shot up along with new house construction and cheap mortgages driven by ultra-low interest rates. It was a classic 'bubble' mentality with everyone jumping on the bandwagon in the hope of making a quick buck. As long as assets were appreciating in value, all was good. US bankers pushed sub-prime mortgages, sometimes offering 100 per cent of the principal, on buyers who were living from pay check to pay check. Bankers invented exotic new financial instruments such as 'credit default swaps' and 'collateralized debt obligations' where cheap mortgages were bundled together, sold and resold, thus spreading the risk – and the potential damage – through the global banking system. When US interest rates were raised to stem inflation in 2007, mortgage payments became too expensive for home owners close to the edge, forcing many into default. House prices began to fall so many people with sub-prime mortgages ended up owing more than their house was worth (sometimes referred to as 'negative equity'). If they defaulted – which they did by the thousands – then lenders had no way of recouping their initial loan. The rising number of defaults pushed many mortgage companies into bankruptcy but the toxic assets also infected US and overseas banks that had bought into the hyper-inflated US mortgage market. With losses mounting and fear spreading, the whole system went into shock and began to shut down. Confidence disappeared. Banks refused to lend to each other; money markets froze; credit dried up and economic growth ground to a halt.

The bursting of the US sub-prime housing bubble brought untold calamity to millions of people around the world. Families lost their homes, their jobs, their

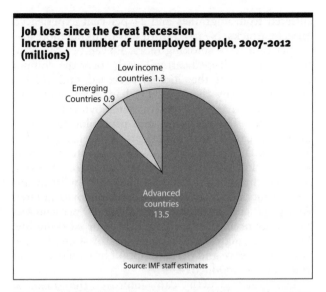

Job loss since the Great Recession
Increase in number of unemployed people, 2007-2012 (millions)

Low income countries 1.3

Emerging Countries 0.9

Advanced countries 13.5

Source: IMF staff estimates

dignity and their self-esteem. According to the IMF, there were 16 million more unemployed in 2012 than in 2007, most of those in industrialized countries. And that figure is surely an underestimation since such data is notoriously unreliable.

Youth unemployment and long-term unemployment are at staggering levels. In 2012, the jobless rate among 15- to 24-year-olds in Western economies was 16.1 per cent, versus 8 per cent for older workers. In Canada it was 15 per cent, twice the national average of 7.2 per cent. In Italy and Sweden it is nudging 25 per cent. But the biggest increase was in Spain, where youth unemployment doubled, from less than 20 per cent in 2008 to almost 40 per cent three years later. Hunger, homelessness, social breakdown and stress-related health and mental-health issues have all increased during the recession. In 2009, a Norwich Union Healthcare survey in Britain found half the 1,000 workers polled had insomnia, a third suffered from migraines and 21 per cent experienced anxiety attacks. Nearly a third was drinking more and 20 per cent were smoking more. Eleven per cent said they were 'self-medicating' with over-the-counter drugs while half the doctors surveyed said alcohol and drug use by their patients had increased.[11] The long-term impact of youth unemployment can be devastating. The economic and psychological consequences – called 'scarring effects' – can last decades. The OECD says failure to solve the problem may lead to a 'lost generation' of angry, disaffected youth, burdened by debt. Not finding a job early in life means you are more likely to experience unemployment later. And you'll end up earning on average 20 per cent less than your peers over the course of your working life. Other 'scarring effects' include loss of skills, limited work experience and the assumption by employers that you'll be less productive.

Economic growth can improve the material conditions of people's lives, especially in the Global South, where millions still live in extreme poverty and lack basic necessities like shelter, healthcare, food and education. But when growth sputters, it's another matter. Those at the bottom are the first to feel the full force of any economic downturn. The problem is compounded by the growing gap between rich and poor and the inexorable concentration of wealth in the hands of the top one per cent – a concern highlighted by the hugely successful 'Occupy' campaigns that spread across North America and Europe in 2011. Even though UN figures show a gradual decline in the number of people living in absolute poverty (about 2.47 billion people in 2008 lived on less than $2 a day compared to 2.59 billion in 1981) the raw numbers are still daunting. There are more people living in poverty today than the total population of the planet a century ago. And despite falling birth rates in many countries – fertility is now at or below replacement level not just in rich countries but also across much of Asia and Latin America – we're still adding a billion people to the global population every 12 years.

Consider this: from 1950 to 2011 the world economy grew more than tenfold, from $7 trillion to $77.2 trillion. It's projected to do the same again by 2050. Before the 2008 global meltdown, the economy was doubling every 15 years, a breathtaking number when you consider that it took all of human history to hit the $7 trillion world economy of 1950. At the same time our insistent mantra of growth-at-all-costs has altered the planet irrevocably. Ecosystems are in decline. We are harvesting natural resources faster than they can be regenerated, colonizing the last wild spaces and pushing non-human species to extinction.

It's time to start questioning our basic assumptions. Are our current economic structures really natural? When does growth become 'uneconomic'? When do the social and environmental costs of unending expansion – dysfunctional and unequal societies, resource depletion, the assault on the natural world, pollution – become so great that they overwhelm the perceived benefits of growth? In the next chapter we'll try to answer some of these vexing questions.

1 worldbank.org/en/country/brazil/overview 2 See interview with Nouriel Roubini by Simon Constable on WSJ Live, nin.tl/171rMmB 3 Stephen Fiddler, 'Firms Cash Hoarding Stunts Europe', Wall Street Journal, 22 Mar 2012. 4 'Threatening a sacred cow: America's fiscal crisis has put defence spending in the crosshairs', The Economist, 10 Feb 2011, nin.tl/194O8AX 5 C Roxburgh/S Lund/J Piotrowski, 'Mapping global capital markets 2011', McKinsey Global Institute, Aug 2011, nin.tl/194Omli 6 F Magdoff/JB Foster, 'What every environmentalist needs to know about capitalism', Monthly Review, Mar 2010. 7 Joseph Stiglitz, 'Adding liquidity is not enough – a fiscal stimulus is needed', The Guardian, 4 Oct 2012. 8 John Maynard Keynes, The General Theory of Employment, Interest and Money, chapter 12. 9 'Global Wage Report 2012/13: Wages and Equitable Growth', International Labour Organization, 7 Dec 2012, nin.tl/171s7pt 10 Paul Sweezy, 'Economic Reminiscences', Monthly Review, May 1995. 11 'Anxiety hitting British workers', BBC News, 29 May 2009, nin.tl/194OuaG

6 GDP and happiness

Measuring wealth by Gross Domestic Product means that the damage done by a hurricane shows up as an economic advantage whereas all kinds of things that we truly value are not measured at all. GDP still rules the economic roost worldwide, yet a range of alternative indicators has recently been developed. Why money does not seem to buy happiness – and why greater equality offers a way forward.

'What you measure affects what you do. If you don't measure the right thing, you don't do the right thing.'
                                                     Joseph Stiglitz

The godfather of green economists, Herman Daly, argues that our world has changed profoundly in the last half century. In the blink of an eye, says Daly, we have moved from an 'empty' planet to a 'full' one. By saying the planet is 'full' Daly is not implying simply that there are too many people – though he does believe that human numbers matter, especially in relation to resource consumption. What he is suggesting is that we have now reached a point in the evolution of the human species where the impact of our *collective economic enterprise* threatens both our own future and the future of the creatures with which we share the planet.

Daly's notion of a 'full' world brings into question what he calls 'uneconomic growth'. That's the apt phrase he chooses to describe the point at which the social and environmental costs of continuous expansion become so great that they overwhelm the perceived benefits. In an 'empty' world we could ignore these costs. But now, in a 'full' world, they threaten our welfare directly.

Prior to the industrial era the world was 'empty' in

the sense that nature was able to handle all that we were able to throw at it. The natural world was bountiful and so vast compared to our human footprint that it was assumed to be infinitely resilient. There seemed to be an enormous gap between what we took from the environment and what appeared available to us. How could the riches of the Earth not be limitless?

And indeed the sheer abundance of the planet was sometimes astounding. When the Italian adventurer Giovanni Caboto (aka John Cabot) sailed the coast of Newfoundland in 1497 he was amazed by the richness of the fishery, reporting that 'the sea there is full of fish that can be taken not only with nets but with fishing baskets'. He would never have divined that 500 years later the cod fishery would collapse with the arrival of factory trawlers, taking with it the economic foundation of the island's unique fishing culture. The same was true of the immense flocks of passenger pigeons whose numbers were so great that they once darkened the skies of North America. Who would have imagined that by 1900 a lethal combination of commercial hunting and habitat loss would drive the bird to extinction? In the push for economic expansion, conquest and settlement, these losses were what modern military strategists might call 'collateral damage' on the great march of human progress.

Specific cultures also occasionally exceeded their local environmental limits and imploded as a result. The anthropologist Joseph Tainter in his book, *The Collapse of Complex Societies*, analyzed the arc of several dynamic, sophisticated peoples including the Mayans and the Romans. His conclusion: complex societies are almost always rigid and inflexible. And it is this complexity and sophistication that is their undoing. They become too inflexible to respond to major social or environmental challenges. Geographer Jared Diamond also touched on this notion in his 2005 book, *Collapse: How Societies Choose to Fail or Succeed*. Diamond looks more specifically at the relationship between vanished cultures and their environment. Why do some complex societies collapse while others survive? One key reason, he suggests, is that failed societies overstep environmental limits by depleting the natural resources on which their survival depends. He cited the famous example of Easter Island, a 164-square-kilometer patch of land in the Pacific Ocean, 3,200 kilometers off the coast of Chile. When Polynesians originally settled the island it was heavily forested. Initially, residents removed trees to build shelters, carve canoes and to cook food. They also used logs to erect the giant, upright stone statues known as *moai* for which the island is famous (some of the statues weigh up to 80 tons and were hauled more than 15 kilometers cross country). This continued for centuries until eventually the last tree was chopped down, a catastrophe which plunged the island into civil war and cannibalism – a self-inflicted societal collapse.

For Diamond, there are striking parallels between the fate of the Easter Islanders and our own current predicament. Our addiction to growth, he implies, is leading us down that same dangerous path to environmental degradation and collapse.

But if this is the case, why do we cheer when the economy is growing and slip into a collective funk when growth fizzles and stops? The simple answer is that we believe it will solve our economic problems, create more jobs, and make people happier. If the pie is bigger, goes the theory, there will be more for everyone. We identify economic growth with social progress and well-being. And we assume that when the economy is expanding we'll become richer and better as a society. In other words we equate growth with development. But of course, they are not the same thing at all. We can have growth (a simple increase in material production) without development (better, happier, more rewarding lives). And we can have development without growth.

The tyranny of GDP

The identification of growth with progress has shaped our economic and social policy for nearly a century. Yet we know now that the logic behind this is badly flawed. In most of the Western world growth is not fostering development; it is subverting it. One problem lies in the key indicator we use to measure progress: Gross Domestic Product, or GDP.

GDP was developed by governments in Britain and the US in the midst of the Great Depression of the 1930s so that governments could get a clear fix on economic production. They were desperate to revive their economies – to put people back to work to spur demand. And with World War Two looming, they were anxious to show their citizens that the economy could manage basic production for both the military and the public. GDP is a way of aggregating data to take a *quantitative* snapshot of the economy. The combined figure represents the total market value of goods and services produced by a country over a fixed period of

---

GNP and GDP measure what can be counted, not what counts

'Our Gross National Product... counts air pollution and cigarette advertising, and ambulances to clear our highways of carnage. It counts special locks for our doors and the jails for the people who break them. It counts the destruction of the redwood and the loss of our natural wonder in chaotic sprawl. It counts napalm and counts nuclear warheads and armored cars for the police to fight the riots in our cities... and the television programs which glorify violence in order to sell toys to our children.

'Yet the Gross National Product does not allow for the health of our children, the quality of their education or the joy of their play. It does not include the beauty of our poetry or the strength of our marriages, the intelligence of our public debate or the integrity of our public officials. It measures neither our wit nor our courage, neither our wisdom nor our learning, neither our compassion nor our devotion to our country, it measures everything, in short, except that which makes life worthwhile.' ∎

Robert F Kennedy, excerpt from a speech at the University of Kansas, 18 March 1968

time. It's usually divided by the population to produce per-capita GDP or the average income per person. The key phrase here is market value: GDP only measures goods and services exchanged for money.

Britain and the US were dominant world powers when the framework of the post-war economic system was hammered out at Bretton Woods, New Hampshire in 1944. So it was inevitable that the two pillars of the new system, the World Bank and the International Monetary Fund, would adopt GDP as a global standard. After World War Two, GDP quickly became part of the UN system of national accounts and was soon applied internationally. (Note: GDP differs from GNP – Gross National Product. GDP counts all the output within a country even if produced by foreign-owned companies, whereas GNP counts economic activity by a country's nationals both inside its borders and abroad. For example, the output of an Australian-owned factory in Britain would be included in Australia's GNP and in Britain's GDP.)

GDP *is* a valuable gauge of overall economic activity. It includes a huge amount of essential data on everything from agricultural production, mining and manufacturing to construction, retail sales and exports. But because it leaves out anything that doesn't have a dollar sign attached, GDP doesn't reflect the entire economy.

As the graphic below illustrates, the economy of goods, services, labor and capital is nested within a larger economy that is not monetized and without which the market system could not function. This wealth includes 'social and cultural capital' – friends, family, cultural heritage, traditional knowledge, community; and 'human capital' – people and their skills, abilities, education, training and health. Beyond this is an outer ring of 'natural capital' which includes both renewable and non-renewable resources.[1]

Natural capital also includes what ecologists call

'ecosystem services'. You may recall that we discussed this concept briefly in Chapter 2. These are the biochemical systems that operate invisibly all around us yet make life possible: examples include the carbon cycle, photosynthesis, pollination of plants, purification of water and waste decomposition. Another kind of important 'capital' – one not included in the diagram – is the physical infrastructure that people have constructed from natural capital over generations. This is sometimes called 'built capital' and includes things like roads, railways, dams, bridges, buildings and telecommunications systems. In this sense 'capital' is like an inherited stock of wealth that contributes to both present and future welfare.

GDP ignores these other layers of capital and this blindness has led to big problems. The largest of these is that GDP treats the depletion of non-renewable

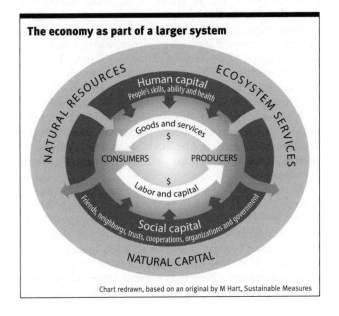

The economy as part of a larger system

NATURAL RESOURCES

ECOSYSTEM SERVICES

Human capital
People's skills, ability and health

Goods and services
$

CONSUMERS   PRODUCERS

$
Labor and capital

Friends, neighborgs, trusts, cooperations, organizations and government

Social capital

NATURAL CAPITAL

Chart redrawn, based on an original by M Hart, Sustainable Measures natural capital as income rather than expenditure. With nothing on the debit side of the ledger, we keep exploiting natural resources as fast as we can harvest them. When coal is strip mined, a forest cleared or farmland destroyed to quarry gravel, the market value of the resource is treated as cash in hand, with no thought given to tomorrow. The same is true of 'ecosystem services'. These systems are priceless yet they lie outside GDP so their destruction counts for nothing. As Herman Daly has written: 'The current national accounting system treats the earth as a business in liquidation.'[2] Despite its limitations, GDP is widely regarded as the single most important measure of human development and well-being. As critics have argued, 'it has become the unchallenged standard and guiding idea in most of our policy-making, politics and public debate about economic development.' Yet, as we've seen, GDP masks far more than it reveals.

Ecological economists argue that growth is now making us poorer instead of richer, especially in the industrialized countries of Europe, North America and Australasia. This 'uneconomic growth' means that we have reached the point where the costs have begun to outstrip the benefits. Unfortunately, we can't look to GDP for proof of this since it only includes the pluses. We need an accounting system that subtracts the negative consequences (the 'bads') from the positive (the 'goods') before we can know for certain that growth is beneficial.

We can easily come up with a long list of 'bads' – though it's not so easy to give them a dollar value. Many people would argue that it's not even appropriate. How do you determine the market value of air that's no longer safe to breathe or a river that has been poisoned by industrial waste? Can you put a price on a ravished mountain top or a hole in the ozone layer? How much is a clear-cut forest worth? Or farmland eroded to desert? Nonetheless, the language of economics is numbers and so it must be done.

This kind of environmental destruction may result from unregulated growth but you won't see it included in any balance sheet. That's because GDP counts only those things that can be bought and sold in the market. Perversely, the negative consequences of growth can

The case against GDP

Distribution: GDP says nothing about how the benefits of growth are distributed. Whether it's up or down, it gives us no sense of who is benefiting or how the average household is faring.

Quantity vs quality: GDP measures the quantity of goods and services but not the quality. Money spent on alcohol and gambling is just as good as money spent on books and exercise.

Defensive expenditures: GDP doesn't distinguish between 'positive' expenditures that increase human welfare and 'defensive' costs like cleaning up pollution or treating socially conditioned diseases (caused by smoking or obesity, for example).

Real economic value vs borrowed and speculative gains: Consumption financed by borrowing adds to GDP just as much as consumption financed by real income gains. Financial services can add to growth by channeling capital to productive investment or by fueling gigantic asset bubbles and speculation.

Depletion of natural capital and ecosystem services: Economic activity that depletes natural resources is just as valuable as economic activity fueled by renewable resources. So burning fossil fuels adds to GDP even while it boosts global warming and threatens massive economic costs in the future as a result of climate change.

Non-market activities: GDP doesn't include 'non-market' services – in the home, in the public sector, in civil society or in the broader ecological systems that surround us. The human and social capital generated by parenting, charity, education, voluntarism, community activities are not measured, even though they affect economic well-being and overall productivity.

Social well-being: GDP doesn't take into consideration social well-being as reflected in rates of poverty, literacy and life expectancy. For example, the US ranks near the top for per-capita GDP but at the same time has the highest poverty and incarceration rates in the advanced world. Likewise, levels of subjective well-being are often higher in poorer countries than in wealthy countries. ■

(Adapted from '*Beyond GDP: new measures for a new economy*', demos.org)

actually rebound and boost growth. Economists call these 'defensive expenditures' – spending that occurs in order to correct a problem. Any natural disaster can turn into a net benefit if it spurs market activity. From a growth perspective, a damaging hurricane or a disastrous flood is a boon since the costs of clean-up will boost GDP. Even illness spurs growth: think of all the healthcare and research dollars churning through the system as a result of disease prevention, research and treatment. The same goes for the millions of hours spent by commuters stopped in traffic, while their car engines burn petrol and pump toxins into the atmosphere. The stress, wasted time and pollution aren't subtracted from GDP but the value of police services, repairing damaged roads and money spent on fuel are added.

Happiness indicators

Despite its obvious failings, GDP is still the go-to metric for economists, finance ministers, corporate CEOs and the business press. But things are changing. There is a growing understanding that GDP gives us a distorted picture of where we want to go as a global community and that we need better, more appropriate, indicators.

One widely quoted initiative is the Human Development Index (HDI), pioneered by the economists Mahbub ul Haq and Amartya Sen for the UN Development Agency. The UNDP has been calculating the HDI for UN members since 1975 and has published the data yearly since 1990 in its *Human Development Report*. The concept is simple: GDP is not an accurate gauge of a country's prosperity or well-being. The HDI combines health and education data with economic data to produce a more subtle and sophisticated view of national development.

In recent years there has been an explosion of interest in new ways of measuring progress. In February

2009, two Nobel Prize-winners, Joseph Stiglitz and Amartya Sen, released the report of the 'Commission on the Measurement of Economic Performance and Social Progress' – an idea hatched by the French government. Their findings stressed the need to move beyond GDP and outlined a series of reforms 'to shift emphasis from measuring economic production to measuring people's well-being'. The Stiglitz/Sen report received little media attention at the time but it did catalyze some political movement. The EU and the OECD now have programs in place to develop alternative indicators. In July 2011 the UN called on member-states to recognize well-being as a 'critical component' of development. And at the June 2012 UN Conference on Sustainable Development in Rio de Janeiro, members endorsed the need for new indicators to complement or replace GDP. That same year Britain decided to create a national happiness index, asking citizens to respond on a scale from zero to ten to questions like: 'How satisfied are you with your life nowadays? How happy did you feel yesterday? To what extent do you feel the things in your life are worthwhile?'[3]

Other countries twigged this even earlier. In 2005 the tiny Himalayan nation of Bhutan (which has a population of just 800,000) decided that Gross National Happiness was more important than Gross National Product. The country's first Gross National Happiness survey was launched in December 2007, followed by a more refined and extensive survey in 2010. Researchers have developed 'nine domains', which they analyze in questionnaires to produce an assessment of the country's well-being. These include health, education, community vitality, psychological well-being, cultural strength, material standard of living, good governance, environmental protection and how people pass their time (work vs leisure inside and outside the home). The government is determined to use the results to shape development and boost overall life satisfaction. And change is happening. Bhutan only opened its borders to the outside world in the 1980s but it has since become an environmental trailblazer.[4] The country is 'carbon neutral', which means it balances the CO_2 it produces with efforts to sequester or store an equal amount of carbon. It has promised to convert all its agriculture to organic production by banning the sale of chemical fertilizers, pesticides and herbicides. It has pledged to protect at least 60 per cent of its forests from logging and it has rejected membership of the World Trade Organization.

'It's easy to mine the land and fish the seas and get rich,' says Bhutan's education minister, Thakur Singh Powdyel. 'Yet we believe you cannot have a prosperous nation in the long run that does not conserve its natural environment or take care of the well-being of its people.'[5]

Ecuador is another poor country that is searching for an alternative to GDP. In 2008 the concept of *buen vivir* was enshrined in the new Ecuadorian constitution. *Buen vivir* is literally translated as 'living well' but that doesn't really capture its full meaning. 'Living well' is about achieving a balance between the human and natural worlds. It's about respect for the environment and respect for people. More controversially, *buen vivir* establishes legal rights for nature and gives the people of Ecuador the authority and the responsibility to enforce those rights. The word used in the constitution is *Pachamama* – an indigenous concept of Mother Earth which reflects spirituality and recognizes that the planet is a self-regulating, living entity. The goal, says the government, is an alternative concept of development with 'an emphasis not on economic growth, but on seeking a balance between human rights and the rights of nature'.

Recognizing the legal rights of nature is a radical

precedent for any government, especially one like Ecuador that depends so heavily on exploiting its rich natural resource base. So it's not surprising that defending *Pachamama* has been a harder slog on the ground. Foreign oil companies are sizing up new discoveries in the Ecuadorian Amazon and mining firms are combing the *altiplano* for gold, copper and silver. The National Collective of Organizations for the Rights of Nature has been leading the fight, working with NGOs and lawyers on a handful of cases. These include a hydroelectric plant that is flooding fertile food land; a shrimp-farming operation that is destroying coastal mangroves; and an open-pit copper mine in the Condor Biosphere Reserve; as well as illegal trafficking and trade in endangered species.[6]

Ecuador also pioneered a unique project in Yasuní National Park, an Amazon rainforest region of unimaginably rich biodiversity. Scientists estimate that a single hectare in Yasuní contains 100,000 insect species, the highest diversity in the world for any plant or animal group. There are more species of trees in one hectare of the Park than in all of North America. As luck would have it, Yasuní also sits on a huge pool of oil – an estimated 920 million barrels worth more than $7 billion. Most Ecuadorians would prefer to leave the rainforest undisturbed, the oil in the ground and the CO_2 that would result from burning the fossil fuel out of the atmosphere.

In 2007, the Andean nation hatched a bold plan to keep the forest intact. They asked the international community to help by pledging half the amount they could earn by selling the oil in the open market: $3.6 billion. Five years later about $300 million had been promised, much of it from smaller countries, individuals and even corporations looking for a public-relations lift. Major oil consumers like Britain and the US refused to pony up. The goal was to raise all $3.6 billion by 2020. But in August 2013, with a paltry $13.3 million in cash in the Yasuní trust fund, Ecuador's President Rafael Correa decided to pull the plug. Some say the pressure from the oil companies and the country's massive debt to China increased pressure to exploit the Park.

The Happy Planet Index and other measures

In addition to these efforts by Bhutan and Ecuador to change the conversation about growth and well-being, a range of other alternative indicators have been developed over the past decade. All go some way to assessing economic performance against the things people actually want: more leisure time, community engagement, good health, decent jobs, affordable housing and resilient natural systems.

Among these indicators are environmental measures like the 'ecological footprint' developed by ecologists William Rees and Mathis Wackernagel (already mentioned in Chapter 4). Footprint accounting keeps track of our ecological assets in the same way a financial balance sheet tracks income and expenditures. An ecological footprint (EF) can be measured for individuals, for cities and for nations. In simple terms it is the area of productive ecosystems required to produce the resources you consume and to absorb the wastes you produce. EFs have been done for most countries around the world.[7] Although results vary dramatically from nation to nation, most wealthy countries are living at the edge, or beyond, the limits of their bio-capacity. They are running ecological deficits – either by eroding their own natural capital; by poaching the bio-capacity of other countries (relying on imports to cover consumption demands); or by using the global commons as a dump for their wastes, especially their CO_2 emissions.

Just as it's possible to spend all our savings and go into debt it's also possible to spend our ecological assets faster than nature can regenerate them. But this kind of deficit spending can't go on forever. Sooner or later we will hit the wall. Current data suggests that our aggregate human eco-footprint is already 40-50 per cent larger than available bio-capacity and that consumption is increasing while our assets are declining. Globally, we are in a state of 'resource overshoot', in essence living off our capital rather than our interest. This is a textbook definition of *unsustainability* – permanently depleting critical natural capital with no thought for the future. 'We have been running annual ecological deficits for at least a quarter of a century,' says the Global Footprint Network. 'As this debt grows, the ecosystems that support our health and our economies are in increasing danger of deterioration or collapse.'[8]

A handful of other alternative indicators are also being developed and refined. These include the Genuine Progress Indicator (GPI) and the Happy Planet Index (HPI). The GPI builds on the Index for Sustainable Economic Welfare (ISEW), which was developed by Herman Daly and Jonathan Cobb in their 1989 book, *For the Common Good*. The GPI uses GDP as its starting point but then makes deductions for things like income inequality, crime and pollution while adding others like the value of housework and volunteer work. It also adjusts for changes in leisure time (the GPI goes up when leisure time increases) and adds in the value of long-lasting consumer products and public infrastructure. (While the money spent on items like fridges and stoves is counted as a cost, the value of the service they provide year after year is included on the credit side of the ledger. This applies equally to public infrastructure like highways, bridges and power stations.) The idea is to measure economic *welfare* as well as economic *activity*.

The GPI was a wake-up call when the data were first released by a group called 'Redefining Progress' in 1995. It focused on the US economy and showed

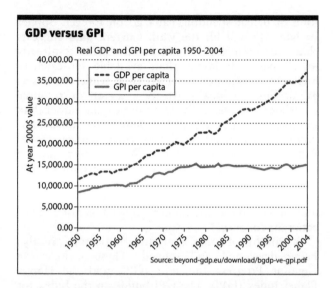

GDP versus GPI

Real GDP and GPI per capita 1950-2004

- - - GDP per capita
— GPI per capita

At year 2000$ value

Source: beyond-gdp.eu/download/bgdp-ve-gpi.pdf

clearly that the GDP emperor wore no clothes. As you can see in the graph above, per-capita GDP steadily climbs between 1950 and 2004. The GPI also improves in tandem from 1950 to about 1974, the golden era of post-war US capitalism, when it begins to level off. Since then per-capita GPI has stagnated at around $15,000 while per-capita income has continued to grow.

What does this growing gap between GDP and GPI mean? At the very least it underlines in a striking way Herman Daly's notion of 'uneconomic growth'. Even though the economy is growing, the genuine progress indicator remains flat. The benefits of growth have been more than offset by the downsides: inequality, pollution, habitat loss, crime, loss of leisure time, depletion of non-renewable resources and more. This enforces the notion that basing policy decisions on the growth of GDP is a losing proposition, inevitably sabotaging movement towards a truly sustainable society.

Britain's innovative New Economics Foundation (NEF) published its first Happy Planet Index (HPI) in 2006, stressing that 'we need to strive for good lives that do not cost the Earth and we need indicators that can help get us there.' The HPI combines two measures of national well-being – life satisfaction and life expectancy – and then divides that number by the country's ecological footprint to produce a final rating. The individual components are themselves revealing. For example, higher life expectancy is generally linked to wealth but not exclusively. Citizens of Chile, Cuba and Costa Rica live nearly as long as people in much richer countries like the US and Japan. The same is true for life satisfaction. Wealthier countries tend to have higher life satisfaction scores but many poorer countries are also near the top. The HPI adds together the top two measures to produce what it calls 'happy life years'. When these figures are plotted against GDP the outcome confirms what other researchers have found: wealth matters but only up to a point. There is what NEF calls 'a clear pattern of diminishing returns'.

Factoring in the environmental footprint can also shift final results dramatically. For example, while the Netherlands' life expectancy and life satisfaction scores are equal to those of the US, it has a footprint half the size, thus putting it much higher in the HPI league table: 67th as opposed to 105th. And while Canada scores near the top for life expectancy and life satisfaction, it plummets down the table to 62nd place as a result of its enormous environmental footprint. The 2012 HPI Report surveys 151 countries (see top 7 and bottom 3 rankings below). Yet the results are perhaps more provocative than useful as a guide to policy decisions. The devil is in the detail. A balance of all three elements is critical to achieve real sustainability. As the report notes: 'The new results confirm that we are still not living on a happy planet. No country is

**2012 Happy Planet Index Rankings
(top 7 and bottom 3)**

Rank	Country	Happy planet index score
1	Costa Rica	64.0
2	Vietnam	60.4
3	Colombia	59.8
4	Belize	59.3
5	El Salvador	58.9
6	Jamaica	58.5
7	Panama	57.8
	World average	**42.5**
149	Qatar	25.2
150	Chad	24.7
151	Botswana	22.6

Source: happyplanetindex.org

able to combine success across the three goals of high life expectancy, high experienced well-being and living within environmental limits.'[9]

Widening of the rich-poor divide

These alternative approaches to measuring progress make it clear that even on its own terms growth isn't working. We avoid talking about the skewed distribution of the planet's wealth and income, dreaming instead that we can grow our way out of the problem. 'A rising tide lifts all boats' is the well-worn cliché. As long as we're growing and producing more wealth, so the argument goes, some of it will eventually trickle down from top to bottom. It's the rationale for letting the rich have their way and the justification for prying markets wide open. The problem is that it's not working. Poverty continues to plague the world while income inequality widens; corporate profits surge and the wealth of the super-rich balloons. *Forbes* magazine tracks the number of billionaires around the world on a yearly basis. There were 1,126 of these super-wealthy in 2012, nearly 20 per cent more than before the financial crisis in 2007. At the top of the heap sits Mexico's telecoms mogul Carlos Slim with a net worth of $69 billion.[10]

More growth may increase per-capita income but GDP doesn't tell us anything about how that income is distributed. This is true between nations as well as within them. There are obscenely wealthy élites in the poorest countries. Even so, average incomes in Europe, North America and Japan are more than 70 times average incomes in low-income countries. In nation after nation the very rich, those at the top of the ladder, are cornering an ever-larger share of the pie. In the US, the world's largest economy, a 2010 study by the Center on Budget and Policy Priorities found that income concentration had reached levels not seen since the 1920s. 'Two-thirds of the nation's total income gains in the economic expansion from 2002 to 2007 flowed to the top 1 per cent of US households, and that top 1 per cent held a larger share of income in 2007 than at any time since 1928.'[11] Meanwhile, the real income of the top 1 per cent grew 10 times faster than the income of the bottom 90 per cent of households. And the US is not alone – most Western nations have followed the same trend. The top 10 per cent of Canadians have seen average incomes rise by 34 per cent over the past 30 years while the bottom 10 per cent have had increases of just 11 per cent. The Ottawa-based Centre for Policy Alternatives reports that the top 1 per cent took almost a third of all income gains from 1997 to 2007.[12] The same holds true for Australia, where there has been a significant increase in inequality since the mid-1990s. The top fifth of households there account for almost 62 per cent of total wealth while the bottom fifth has just 0.9 per cent. Those same 20 per cent also increased their average net worth by 15 per cent from 2005-10, while the bottom fifth saw a rise of only 4 per cent.[13] The Scandinavian countries of Denmark, Finland, Norway and Sweden have the most equal income distribution in the West. But even there inequality is on the rise.

In the two fastest-growing economies of the South – China and India – inequality is also a concern. China has experienced the world's highest growth rates in recent decades but it is hobbled by endemic corruption and widening income inequality. In October 2012 *The New York Times* reported that 'many relatives' of China's prime minister, Wen Jiabao, had joined the super-rich during his time in power. The paper noted that 'the prime minister's relatives – some of whom, including his wife, have a knack for aggressive deal making' – controlled assets worth at least $2.7 billion.'[14] In 2007 the Chinese scholar Minxin Pei estimated that corruption was costing the country three per cent of its GDP, equivalent to about $200 billion today. And, according to *Bloomberg News,* the extended family of China's new President, Xi Jinping, has assets of nearly $500 million, including Hong Kong real estate worth $55.6 million.[15]

Despite two decades of breakneck growth, the gap between rich and poor is widening. Communist Party leaders are understandably worried that mounting social unrest may threaten the whole system. Nearly 200 million poorly paid migrant workers provide the muscle for the country's huge export sector and their clout is increasing. They are demanding higher wages and better working conditions. Strikes, protests and demonstrations have become routine across the country. The Chinese Academy of Social Sciences reports that strikes in 2011 were 'better organized, more confrontational and more likely to trigger copycat action'. It appears that millions of Chinese workers are fed up, no longer willing to make sacrifices for the national good while Party *apparatchiks* and their cronies enjoy the high life. They are clamoring for their fair share of the benefits of economic growth.

Under pressure from boosters of economic globalization (local élites, foreign corporations and many Western governments) India opened its economy to market forces in the early 1990s. Initially, growth in the world's second most populous nation (more than 1.2 billion people) accelerated. GDP growth averaged over 8 per cent between 2004 and 2011. From 1996 to 2012 the country's per-capita income shot up from $400 to $1,400. It is estimated that India's middle class will expand by 50 million people yearly in the coming decades.

Visible signs of wealth are everywhere in the booming cities. The streets of the capital, Delhi, are so clogged with imported Japanese, American and European cars that air pollution has reached deadly levels. According to the *New York Times*, fine-particulate pollution has risen by 47 per cent in the last decade, while nitrogen-oxide levels have increased by 57 per cent. There are now more than seven million motor vehicles in Delhi, a jump of 65 per cent since 2003. Another 1,400 new cars and trucks are added daily.[16] India has also joined the billionaires' club. There are 48 of them in *Forbes* 2012 list. The country's richest person, Mukesh Ambani, has a personal fortune of $22.3 billion.

But spectacular GDP growth has not benefited the majority: two out of three Indians live in crushing poverty. The rural economy has collapsed. Millions are fleeing the land while hunger is increasing. A report by the International Food Policy Research Institute found that the proportion of hungry people in India has actually increased since 1996. 'India's track record is disappointing,' the authors wrote, since 'generally, higher incomes are associated with less hunger'.[17] A 2011 study by the OECD, meanwhile, found that income inequality has doubled over the past two decades. The top 10 per cent of wage-earners now make 12 times more than the bottom 10 per cent, whereas in 1990 they made 6 times more. India has the highest number of poor people in the world – 42 per cent of Indians live on less than $1.25 a day.[18] According to UNICEF, 44 per cent of Indian children under five are underweight and 48 per cent are stunted.

And so it goes. The richest 80 per cent of the world's population consumes the lion's share of the world's resources while the poorest 20 per cent get by on just 1.5 per cent of global output. And the ratios are getting worse. Growth becomes an excuse for continued

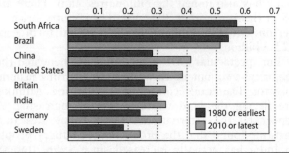

What is the Gini coefficient?

This is the most commonly used measure of income inequality, developed by Italian statistician and demographer, Corrado Gini, in 1921. The Gini coefficient is measured on a scale of 0 to 1. A Gini number of 0 represents exact equality which means that everyone has the same amount of income. A Gini coefficient of 1 represents total inequality, where one person has all the income and the rest have none.

Growing income inequality (selected countries)
Gini co-efficient measure of inequality

South Africa
Brazil
China
United States
Britain
India
Germany
Sweden

■ 1980 or earliest
■ 2010 or latest

inequality: why confront the issue if we can simply grow our way out of the problem? Over-consumption by the rich is justified by marginal increases in wealth for the poor while relative poverty stays the same or increases.

Even the middle class is feeling the pinch. Incomes were rising and social safety nets expanding during the bubbling post-War years (1950-80). In the industrialized nations, the middle class grew and prospered. That era has now ended. Well-paid union jobs are vanishing, unemployment has crept into the double-digit range and personal debt has exploded. Globalization and the pressure to increase productivity have driven down wages and fueled a race to the bottom. Corporate leaders and their acolytes in the business press babble on endlessly about the need to become 'more competitive'. Yet working people across Europe and North America have seen what being 'competitive' means in practice: government bail-outs for big banks and corporations, stagnant or lower wages, reduced benefits, higher unemployment, declining government services and crumbling infrastructure.

Companies trim costs by dismissing workers and closing plants, boosting profits in the process. Unemployment increases while governments slash social-welfare programs. Still, growth works for some. The top 500 global corporations reported record revenues of $29.5 trillion in 2011, up 13.2 per cent from the previous year. And banks in both Europe and North America posted record profits.[19] US banks in 2012 recorded their highest earnings since the 2007-09 financial crisis, according to the Federal Deposit Insurance Corporation. Earnings jumped nearly 20 per cent from 2011 to the second highest on record at $141.3 billion.[20] Meanwhile, the UK's largest bank, HSBC Holdings, cleared $16.79 billion in 2011 amidst plans to slash 30,000 jobs globally.

Why money does not buy happiness

Recent history shows that the fruits of economic growth have been unequally distributed and that mass poverty and damaging unemployment are more worrisome than ever. But what is equally important is that, beyond a certain critical point, getting richer doesn't seem to make us happier.

How could that be? Everyone dreams of living on easy street, winning the lottery and having no financial worries. As the old adage attributed to Mae West goes: 'I've been rich and I've been poor; believe me, rich is better.' While this makes common sense, sociologists and economists have discovered a more complex relationship between wealth, material consumption and life satisfaction. The British scholar Richard Layard was one of those who pioneered the field of 'happiness studies'. Layard discovered a 'threshold effect' in respect of happiness and income. For example, he found that, although per-capita income in the US has tripled since 1950, the percentage of people who say they are very happy has remained virtually flat. Other studies have confirmed those findings across the industrialized world. It seems that money does buy happiness, but only up to a point. Beyond that, as GDP increases, you may be richer but you won't be any happier. Layard found that once basic needs and essential creature comforts were met, additional income growth did not boost life satisfaction. You might call this the law of diminishing returns.

There are a couple of reasons why this appears to be the case. Part of the answer lies in what's been called the 'hedonic treadmill' – an academic turn of phrase which means that the emotional wallop of material possessions is short-lived. Once people become accustomed to a higher standard of living, their satisfaction soon levels off and they wind up back at Layard's 'threshold' again. The end result is that richer doesn't mean happier, though people still run ever faster on the treadmill, desperately striving for more money to buy more things in search of that elusive goal. Aspirations, it seems, are endless but habituation is always around the corner.

Another explanation for why growth fails to boost happiness is the idea of 'positional goods'. The logic here is that, because we are 'social beings', material consumption only increases our happiness in relation to others. So it's *relative* rather than *absolute* consumption that's important. If everyone's income rises (or at least those people who count) then you're really no better off – what matters is not 'keeping up with the Joneses' but staying ahead of them.

The British economist Fred Hirsch explored this notion in his book, *The Social Limits to Growth*. Hirsch wrote his study in the 1970s, before the forces of economic globalization were unleashed and when the world was a somewhat kinder and gentler place. Nonetheless, like his North American counterpart John Kenneth Galbraith, he was perplexed by 'the paradox of affluence'. Why was growth so important, he wondered, if it didn't actually make us more satisfied? As Hirsch wrote: 'When people become richer compared with other people, they become happier. But when whole societies have become richer, they have not become happier...'

For Hirsch, 'positional goods' were the key to understanding why economic growth doesn't lead to increased well-being in industrialized nations. Hirsch made a clear distinction between 'material goods' and 'positional goods'. By positional goods he meant possessions that gain their value only when other people don't have them. This has to do with social status. The US economist Thorstein Veblen was one of the first academics to link social status with material consumption in his ground-breaking 1899 book, *The Theory of the Leisure Class*. Veblen coined the term 'conspicuous consumption' to refer to people who buy things not because they're useful but because they want to display their wealth and social standing. In some ways this is common sense. In all pre-capitalist societies, from the Egyptians to the Aztecs, dominant élites have used material possessions – precious gems, jewelry, elaborate clothing – to indicate their status and privilege. But in Veblen's view consumer behavior in a capitalist economy was radically different. The two were intimately linked through mass production; eventually the price of luxury goods would fall, thus making them widely available. Unlike pre-industrial societies, this ensured that conspicuous consumption became a never-ending treadmill. The 'leisure class', outfoxed by mass production, would be constantly on the hunt for new luxury goods to use as status symbols.

This dovetails with Hirsch's view of 'positional goods', which also hinges on status. The logic works like this. If I'm the only person on my street with a $200,000 Mercedes-Benz automobile, that reflects my income and sets me apart. But if everyone is suddenly driving a new luxury vehicle then I'm nothing special. I've now got to splash out on another big-ticket item if I want to win my status back. The value of positional goods is diminished when others have them. Education is another good example. It's the scarcity of an Oxbridge degree that gives it social (and market) value. The same is true of a peaceful summer cottage on a quiet northern lake. When the shoreline begins to look like a crowded suburb and buzzing jet boats take over, the dream begins to fade. Competition for positional goods makes them less desirable.

Alternatively, 'material goods' are those which still have value no matter how many others have them. There is no status lost if all my friends wear warm boots and a thick coat in the winter; or if my neighbor and I both own backyard barbeques.

Hirsch concluded that, as economies grow and

societies become wealthier, more and more consumer activity is fixed on positional goods. These goods then flatten the benefits of growth because jousting for social position is essentially a 'zero sum' game: my gain is your loss, and vice versa. If I buy something to gain status and then you buy the same thing, I'm no better off. We continue to chase wealth but we're no farther ahead. Which begs the question: if we're getting richer but not getting happier – and wrecking the planet in the process – what's the point?

Occupy Wall Street

Growing inequality and the concentration of wealth and power in the hands of a tiny minority was the focus of Occupy Wall Street (OWS), a movement which spread rapidly across the US, Canada and Europe in the autumn of 2011. 'We are the 99%' was their rallying slogan, a phrase that summed up widely felt frustration with an economic system seen to be failing the vast majority while big banks and private corporations were bailed out with public funds. It was

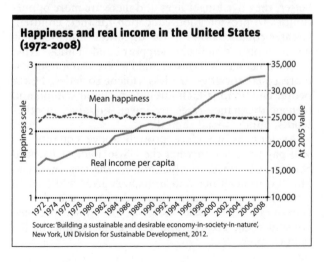

Happiness and real income in the United States (1972-2008)

Source: 'Building a sustainable and desirable economy-in-society-in-nature', New York, UN Division for Sustainable Development, 2012.

suddenly as if the old excuse for continued growth was now exposed. The system was built on the belief that, as long as the economy is growing, we don't need to worry about distribution. There would be more for everyone, eventually. But now the cat was out of the bag. Not only is growth not making people happier but it is also making inequality worse.

A year before the Occupy movement swept the globe, a remarkable study by British epidemiologists Richard Wilkinson and Kate Pickett reinforced the notion that equality should trump growth as the key focus of government policy. Their book, *The Spirit Level*, looks at the social consequences of income inequality, analyzing more than 30 countries using data from the UN, OECD and elsewhere. Their conclusions? Health and social problems are worse in more unequal countries and more equality benefits everyone – not just those at the bottom of the income ladder. The upshot of this is that more equal societies are stronger and more cohesive. Community is stronger. People are happier, their mental health is better; they live longer lives and there are more opportunities to provide good education for their children. Greater equality bows in the direction of democracy, which bolsters mutual support and builds trust between people. Wilkinson and Pickett also found that more equal societies are less violent societies. Fewer people end up in jail, children do better at school, and teenage pregnancy rates are lower. Equality, in other words, builds 'social capital'.

As long as we place growth above equality we will pay the price in what the US sociologist Richard Sennett described as the 'hidden injuries of class'. Shorter, unhealthier and unhappier lives addicted to a mindless consumerism that is depleting the planet's resources. We'll look more at the links between consumerism, growth and ecological decline in the next chapter.

1 All raw materials are non-renewable if used unwisely. But a renewable resource is one that *potentially* renews itself faster than the rate at which humans might exploit it; things like the marine fishery, farm land, forests and animal protein. Renewable *energy* sources include solar, geothermal and wind power. Non-renewable resources include fossil fuels, minerals and fresh water aquifers. **2** Cited in Clifford Cobb, Ted Halstead, and Jonathan Rowe, 'If the GDP is up, why is America down?' *The Atlantic*, Oct 1995. **3** Randeep Ramesh, 'Good neighbours and green spaces make happier Britons', *Guardian Weekly*, 30 Nov 2012. **4** For details see Bhutan's Gross National Happiness Commission, gnhc.gov.bt **5** Annie Kelly, 'Gross national happiness in Bhutan: the big idea from a tiny state that could change the world', *The Observer*, 1 Dec 2012. **6** Natalia Greene, 'Rights of Nature: An Update on Ecuador', *Rights of nature: planting real seeds of change*, Global Exchange, 2012. **7** For specific country results see footprintnetwork.org/en/index.php/GFN **8** 'The Ecological Wealth of Nations', Global Footprint Network, 2010. **9** See latest results at happyplanetindex.org **10** forbes.com/billionaires/list **11** H Shaw/C Stone, 'Tax data show richest 1 per cent took a hit in 2008 but income remained highly concentrated at the top', Center on Budget and Policy Priorities, 21 Oct 2010. **12** nin.tl/1aMnsnX **13** socialinclusion.gov.au/home **14** David Barboza, 'Billions in Hidden Riches for Family of Chinese Leader', *New York Times*, 25 Oct 2012. **15** nin.tl/1aMnHPS **16** Niharika Mandhana, 'Untamed Motorization Wraps an Indian City in Smog', *New York Times*, 26 Dec 2012. **17** *2012 Global Hunger Index,* nin.tl/1gjRB50 **18** OECD, *Divided We Stand: Why Inequality Keeps Rising*, Dec 2011, nin.tl/1aMo1ya **19** nin.tl/1gjRMNQ **20** Emily Stephenson, 'US banks post highest profits since 2006', *Financial Post*, 26 Feb 2013.

7 Life on the treadmill

How shopping has become both therapy and religion – and how advertising has taken us deeper into a world built on consumerism and waste. Where once we dreamed that technology would liberate us from work, those in work are having to work harder and longer to afford the latest 'stuff' while rates of unemployment rise. Sharing out the available work more equally could represent a way forward.

'I'm all lost in the supermarket; I can no longer shop happily. I came in here for the special offer, guaranteed personality.'

The Clash

The Friday following the national Thanksgiving holiday in the United States is a day of intense contemplation and ritual. More than 300 million Americans rise in the pre-dawn hours, groggy from too much food and drink, slide into their cars and hit the road, ready to partake in a mass communal ceremony.

They're going shopping.

It's 'Black Friday', the biggest sales day of the year for US retailers. (It's called 'black' Friday because sales that day are said to put retailers' accounts into the 'black' for the rest of the year.) Store managers prepare weeks in advance, training employees for the invasion. Shoppers queue in the middle of the night in anticipation of cut-rate bargains. Some pitch tents. Parking lots are jammed. The competition for sale-priced goods is so intense that fights frequently break out. According to 2012 press reports, one shopper at a Kmart in Sacramento, California, threatened to stab people while waiting in line for the doors to open. In Los Angeles, police helicopters hovered above malls while officers on bikes and horses patrolled the pavements.

In San Antonio, Texas, a queue jumper hid behind a refrigerator after a fellow shopper pulled a gun on him. The previous year, a Michigan woman looking to snag discounted video games zapped her competitors with pepper spray, sending dozens to hospital. The US National Retail Federation estimates that shoppers in 2012 spent an average of $423 each on Black Friday while total spending for the four-day Thanksgiving weekend topped $59 billion, up 13 per cent from the previous year.[1]

Black Friday is a frenzied explosion of consumer culture. But it's unique only in that it's a concentrated burst of buying designed by merchants to focus and stimulate sales over a few days. For most people today, consumerism is a 365-day event. No matter where we go, we are met with advertisements and sales pitches. Risqué lingerie ads cover the side of public buses, cinemas assault you with 10 minutes of ads before the film starts, pop-ups litter your computer screen and telemarketers clog the phone lines. The jerseys of professional footballers are festooned with corporate logos. Even the space above the urinal in the local pub is fair game. It is almost impossible to escape the siren call of commerce. But it hasn't always been that way.

Before the era of mass production, people were employed to produce the goods and services that the public needed. But the modern industrial process has changed that forever. Today things are topsy-turvy. The global economy produces way too much stuff, not because we *need* it but because we need *to sell* it. A lot of what is produced for the consumer market is unnecessary and much of it useless. Our closets are crammed with clothes; our basements, garages and attics are jammed with junk we can't remember why we bought in the first place. We go on churning out mountains of stuff because it's good for growth and people need jobs. We need to keep buying things to keep the economy moving. But in the process we're trashing the planet, burning through tons of non-renewable resources, destroying the last vestiges of wilderness and knowingly altering the earth's climate. Growth has become our faith and consumerism our credo.

The illusion of consumer power

But does consumerism spur growth or does the economic system's built-in need for growth drive consumerism? Mainstream economists believe that consumers are 'sovereign' in the marketplace. In other words, our wants, needs and greed are what shape production. Business simply responds to our demands. It follows that if consumers really are 'sovereign' then we have the power to change our behavior if we know it's causing problems. This is the thinking behind 'green consumerism'. If we buy only things whose making won't harm the planet – 'green' eco-friendly products – then business will respond to these 'market signals' and reshape the production process to build a sustainable world.

Unfortunately, it is not so easy. There's no evidence that simply changing buying habits will de-rail the growth machine. Of course, developing an eco-conscience is laudable and choosing to 'buy green' is an important personal commitment to change. But the global market is just too big and too complex for individual buying decisions to make much of an impact.

The influential liberal economist John Kenneth Galbraith called the idea of consumer sovereignty an 'innocent fraud' masking the economic power of all-powerful private corporations who really control the market. Galbraith, who first examined modern consumer culture in his 1958 book, *The Affluent Society*, concluded that production drives consumption, not the other way round. Advertising creates the 'craving for more elegant automobiles, more exotic food, more erotic clothing, more elaborate entertainment' and 'production only fills a void that it has itself created'.[2] Today, advertising is a billion-dollar worldwide industry. We'll take a closer look inside that world in a moment. But first let's explore Galbraith's idea that 'production only fills a void that it has itself created'.

As we discovered in Chapter 5, the relentless drive for profits and growth is built into modern industrial economies. Both are fundamental to the system's success. As one wag put it: 'Capitalism is like a bicycle; when you stop peddling, it falls over.' Competition fuels a continuous drive for efficiency, which in turn boosts production (often to the point of excess). Reduced costs lead to higher margins and increased profits. But in a fundamental sense the system is too efficient for its own good, producing more goods than the market can handle. High levels of consumption are needed to keep the bicycle upright; otherwise the thing may wobble and crash, with dire consequences. This was glaringly evident by the early 1920s, when factories were able to produce vastly more than people could buy. Galbraith argued that, like growth and profits, consumerism is also woven into the fabric of industrial production. Faced with bulging inventories, there is no alternative but to convince people to buy more stuff.

Luckily, a solution was at hand: advertising. As the sociologist, Stuart Ewen, points out in his 1976 classic, *Captains of Consciousness, Advertising and the Social Roots of Consumer Culture*, when Henry Ford introduced 'assembly-line production' in 1910 at his plant in Highland Park, Michigan, it took 12 hours and 22 minutes to assemble one automobile. By the spring of 1914, the plant was churning out 1,000 vehicles a day and it took workers just an hour and 33 minutes to assemble one car. Between 1860 and 1920, new technology resulted in massive increases in productivity. US industrial output increased by a factor of 12. Population also boomed; in fact it tripled but, even so, it was impossible for the market to absorb the sudden glut of mass-produced goods. So, writes Ewen, 'it became imperative to invest the laborer with a financial power and psychic desire to consume'. Ewen goes further, emphasizing how advertising and the invention of consumer credit ('buying on the instalment plan') not only boosted sales but also shifted the focus of worker discontent from the 'sphere of production' to the 'sphere of consumption'. Class conflict was redirected from the shop floor to the marketplace, where tensions were dissolved through a 'democracy of goods'.

The explosion of advertising

In his book, *Advertising the American Dream*, the historian Roland Marchand suggests that the goal of early advertising was the flattening of class differences. The explicit message was that everyone could aspire to material possessions that were once available only to the rich. It didn't matter if you were gentry, *nouveau riche* or a working stiff – you could drink the same coffee, use the same laundry detergent, brush with the same toothpaste or sleep on the same mattress. That was the beauty of mass production. 'The social message of the parable of the Democracy of Goods was clear,' writes Marchand. 'Antagonistic envy of the rich was unseemly; programs to redistribute wealth were unnecessary. The best things in life were already available to all at reasonable prices... Incessantly and enticingly repeated, advertising visions of fellowship in a Democracy of Goods encouraged Americans to look to similarities in consumption styles rather than to political power or control of wealth for evidence of significant equality.'

The modern advertising industry exploded in the 1920s as mass production spread. Business needed to convince people to buy more and advertising was the key, playing on human insecurities, fears and desires. Writer Vance Packard referred to advertisers as 'merchants of discontent' who offered people status, happiness and fulfilment through consumption. In his 1957 book, *The Hidden Persuaders*, Packard revealed how advertisers exploited the weaknesses of the human psyche, selling not just products but brands and 'brand personalities'. Today, advertising is more sophisticated and even more ubiquitous. Market researchers slice and dice reams of esoteric data to determine how to entice buyers to open their wallets. And our new 24/7 digital world is a goldmine: cellphones, credit cards and computers leave a trail of readily available information. Analysts can track a person's buying patterns and behavior (known as 'history sniffing' and 'behavior sniffing' according to ex-ad exec Martin Lindstrom) and then use that information to figure out what other things to sell you.

Children are an especially important market. They are targeted early in the belief that habits learned at a young age will last a lifetime. In the US alone, advertising aimed at kids is worth more than $12 billion a year.[3] Next time you walk down the aisle of your local supermarket, take a look at the products shelved at the eye level of a six-year-old. No wonder the average American child can recognize more than 100 brands by the age of three and more than 300 by the time they are 10.

But it's not just children, of course. All of us are targets. The main goal of advertising is to nurture acquisitive urges, to plant a desire for more: possessions,

---

A $500-billion business

The global ad business was worth more than $500 billion in 2012. TV was the top draw with more than 40 per cent of all ad revenue, while internet ad sales continued to boom. The US is the biggest advertising market, with 2012 spending of around $166 billion.[4] ■

An advertising desert

There is something unusual about Havana. You sense it when you first arrive, though it's hard to put your finger on it. Cuba's grand but crumbling old capital is a jewel. The faded colonial architecture in the city center is glorious. T-shirt-clad tourists wander the busy streets. Lumbering taxis, made-in-Detroit relics from the 1950s, cruise for business while locals crowd into ugly *camelos*, articulated buses belching diesel fumes. Street vendors hawk their wares; laughing schoolkids in crisp uniforms joust and tease. It all seems normal and then it hits you: most shop windows are empty. But it's not the shortage of consumer goods that's odd. It's the fact that there is no commercial advertising. Yes, there are propaganda posters of Che, Fidel Castro and other revolutionary heroes. But there are no billboards, no posters and no gaudy neon signs selling soft drinks, cell-phones, cosmetics or cars. It's an advertising desert – refreshing but also unworldly, kind of like stepping onto another planet. Cuba has its share of problems – a shortage of basic consumer products is one of them. But it must be one of the last places on Earth not inundated by the ubiquitous urgings of corporate culture to buy more stuff. ■

beauty, happiness, sex, acceptance, love. Advertisers promise all these things. But it is a one-way conversation that clogs all media: radio, TV, film, newspapers, magazines, billboards, flyers and online via mobile phones, tablets and laptops. We see and hear advertising messages thousands of times a day. But we are passive recipients. There is nowhere to hide, nowhere to run.

We have become so habituated to the siren call of commerce that it has receded to background noise, yet the messages still hammer away at our psyche. Gradually, marketing noise and the clamor of buy-and-sell have penetrated our communities, our politics and our public spaces (including the airwaves). The sophisticated psychological techniques advertisers use to sell deodorant, cars and beer are now widely used to sell politicians. Like the marketing of consumer goods, the selling of politicians is more about feelings and emotions than ideas or policies. We vote for them because they seem 'honest' or 'trustworthy' or 'tough-minded'. Politicians are packaged as celebrities or performers and sold for their invented personalities. Media critics refer to this as the 'colonization of consciousness', where the steady drumbeat of the sales pitch warps our worldview.

As much as we would like to think we are immune to advertising, we are not. Once marketing messages enter your brain you cannot erase them. According to culture critic and former advertising executive Jerry Mander: 'Images ride a freeway into your brain and remain there permanently. No thought is involved. Every advertiser knows this. As a viewer, you may sometimes say, "I don't believe this," but the image remains anyway.'

Much of this saturation happens via television. Here's how Mander sums up the impact of TV advertising in the US, noting that the situation in the rest of the industrialized world is little different:

> *According to the Nielsen Company... 99 per cent of American homes have television sets and 95 per cent of the population watches at least some television every day. Two-thirds of US homes have three or more sets, arranged for separate, private viewing. The average home has a TV playing for about seven hours per day, even when no-one is watching. While the average adult watches about five hours per day, the average child aged two to eleven watches nearly four hours per day. The average adult over age sixty-five watches about seven hours per day...*
>
> *The average television viewer watching television for four-plus hours per day is hit with about 25,000 commercials per year, and by age 65, that number exceeds two million. That would be 25,000 annual repetitions of basically the same message: You will be happier if you buy something.[5]*

Advertising manipulates and seduces. But those dreams may soon turn to nightmares. Many of the must-have items that we buy as symbols of the good life are designed to have a short shelf life. Toys, kitchen appliances and sporting goods soon fall apart, wind up in the nearest landfill and need to be replaced, all of which boosts growth. This is what business analysts call 'planned obsolescence' – goods are designed to wear out. The global computer firm, Apple, recently came under fire in Brazil for alleged planned obsolescence. The Institute of Politics and Law (IBDI) launched a legal battle against the company, claiming it could have included all the tech upgrades from its iPad 4 when it launched the third-generation iPad just seven months earlier. Lawyer Sergio Palomares told Brazil's *Jornal do Comérciao*, 'Consumers thought [they were] buying high-end equipment, not knowing [it] was already an obsolete version.'[6]

More familiar to most of us is 'perceived obsolescence' – when we're convinced that our possessions are just not up to par any more, even if they're not worn out or broken. Things quickly pop in and out of fashion. A TV or laptop computer more than a few years old is clunky and dated. Last year's jeans seem old-fashioned. Passenger cars can now run efficiently for a decade or more. Yet manufacturers release new models every year, constantly tweaking the design to make older models seem dowdy and tired. The wheel of production and consumption keeps spinning, heedless of the enormous economic, environmental and social costs.

Damage to community

It's no coincidence that the rise of consumer culture has mirrored significant social shifts over the past century. In the West, especially, age-old bonds of community have become tattered and frayed as a result of massive economic and cultural upheaval. The notion of 'the public' as a shared community of mutual support has been supplanted by a rough-hewn individualism where people look to their own interests first. Much of what was once public life has become privatized. Technology has revolutionized transport and communications so that the world has literally become the 'global village' that Canadian media analyst Marshall McLuhan predicted half a century ago. We can hop on a plane and be on the other side of the world in a matter of hours. We talk to friends or work colleagues in Europe or Asia as if they were next door. But the glue that once held us together has weakened. Families are torn apart when children work hundreds or thousands of miles away. Traditional religious institutions, once a focus of family and community life, have lost their cohesive force as secularism gains ground. We spend long hours commuting in automobiles, cocooned from our fellow travelers. And when we're not in our cars we spend more and more of our time staring at computer and television screens, at work and at home for entertainment. The spread of car-dependent suburbs and 'edge cities' has left people physically isolated and disconnected from age-old forms of community. The traditional city model of urban density has morphed into an extended plane of uniformity interrupted by strip malls and six-lane commuter speedways. Giant shopping complexes flanked by vast parking lots function as 'town centers'.

The US sociologist Robert D Puttman, in his book *Bowling Alone*, outlines what he calls the erosion of 'social capital' in post-War America. He does not extend his analysis to the rest of the industrialized world but it's clear that these same modernizing tendencies are at work in Europe and elsewhere. The notion of 'social capital' was raised in the last chapter when we looked at how traditional methods of measuring the market economy (such as GDP) ignore substantial parts of our economic life. Puttman uses the term in much the same way – as a phrase that captures those multi-layered relationships woven from friendship, collegiality and community that both root us and satisfy fundamental human needs for connection and meaning. To a large extent, this loss of social capital has been replaced by a 'culture of consumerism' where people replace their hunger for social relationships with commodity relationships. The market expands to fill the void.

Karl Marx explored this in the first volume of his classic treatise, *Capital,* where he introduced the term 'commodity fetishism' to describe the separation of goods from the process of producing them. 'The wealth of societies in which the capitalist mode of production prevails appears as an immense collection of commodities,' he wrote. Marx believed that in a capitalist economy commodities took on a life of their own, imbued with symbolic meaning. This 'fetishism', he said, disguised the true function of commodity production, elevating 'exchange value' above 'use value'. For Marx this preoccupation with things was a diversion from the real problem – the fundamental gap in power and wealth between the capitalist and the worker. Today's fixation on consumer culture would for him be a logical extension of this fetishism.

Nearly a century later the German-American philosopher, Herbert Marcuse, drew on Marx for inspiration in his influential 1964 book, *One Dimensional Man*:

> We are again confronted with one of the most vexing aspects of advanced industrial civiliza-tion: the rational character of its irrationality. Its productivity and efficiency, its capacity to increase and spread comforts, to turn waste into need, and destruction into construction, the extent to which this civilization transforms the object world into an extension of man's mind and body makes the very notion of alienation questionable. The people recognize themselves in their commodities;

they find their soul in their automobile, hi-fi set, split-level home, kitchen equipment. The very mechanism which ties the individual to his society has changed, and social control is anchored in the new needs which it has produced.

Is it any wonder then that shopping has become a central preoccupation of modern life? It is so pervasive that millions of people shop for entertainment or simply to make themselves feel better, a process psychologists call 'retail therapy'. A recent survey by a major Canadian bank found that 59 per cent of Canadians are impulse shoppers who hit the malls 'to cheer themselves up'. As the saying goes, 'When the going gets tough, the tough go shopping'. On average, Canadian shoppers spend $310 a month on things they want, but don't need – and most of them later regret it. Researchers have found that this kind of binge shopping produces a quick shot of pleasure that quickly fades into guilt, shame and disappointment. And then there are the practical concerns. A third of shoppers use credit to finance their purchases and many end up in debt as a result. Total household debt across the West has ballooned in the past 30 years to previously unimaginable levels. In Canada, for example, the debt-to-income ratio topped 165 per cent in early 2013, just 10 points below the peak reached in the US prior to the 2008 housing crash.[7] (The collapse of the housing market increased household debt. Without work people were unable to keep up with mortgage payments even as the market value of their property tumbled. Tens of thousands lost their homes while others wound up in a position of 'negative equity' where the amount owing on the mortgage was greater than the market value of the house.)

The irony is that while powerful financial markets fret about 'wasteful' public spending and 'dangerous' levels of private debt, economic growth itself depends on credit. Debt provides both the means and the motive for economic expansion. 'Spend, spend, spend' is the mantra we hear whenever the economy goes slack. We are urged to spend lavishly at every turn. Big banks and major retailers flog credit cards and low-interest credit lines with abandon. When markets collapse and demand slumps, consumers are urged to open their wallets to boost growth. It's a little like the *Goldilocks* fairy tale where the perfect porridge is neither 'too hot nor too cold'. Too much debt clogs the system and too little brings it to a halt. The logic is perverse and can lead to what economists call 'adverse feedback loops'. If families put aside money to pay down debt this will help the household budget. But in the wider economy it can actually make things worse by squeezing overall demand for goods. Output falls, which means that fewer workers are needed to produce those goods. That leads to more unemployment and even less market demand. That in turn forces more people to try to reduce their debt load. It's a familiar downward spiral.

It's at this point that governments typically intervene to provide fiscal stimulus to kick start the economy and get people back to work. This is the familiar Keynesian approach of 'pump priming' via deficit-financed government spending that we saw after the crisis of 2008. As long as lawmakers were allowed to spend public funds on new infrastructure, this tack was successful. An all-out economic collapse was avoided and new jobs were created. Even so, billions in stimulus spending was not enough to soak up the surplus labor. Many of the jobs that have been created are part-time and poorly paid. Young people, especially, are unable to find satisfying work at a decent wage. Recent moves in the European Union have made things worse. The new orthodoxy of austerity has seen governments slash spending and cut social services while thousands of public-sector workers have been laid off, bleeding even more demand from the system. A report by the International Labour Organization (ILO) notes there are nearly 200 million unemployed worldwide and another 40 million who have given up hope of finding a job. 'The youth unemployment rate,' the report continues, 'is expected to increase to 12.9 per cent by 2017; some 35 per cent of all young unemployed have been out of a job for six months or longer in advanced economies, up from 28.5 per cent in 2007.'[8]

Too little work – and too much

Joblessness is more than just a lack of income. It also blocks the path to community participation, social purpose and self-respect. Yet modern working life is highly schizophrenic. Millions of people work punishingly long hours, 50 hours a week and more, while others have no paid employment at all. For countless employees, the digital revolution has created a workplace without walls. People can analyze spreadsheets, send text messages or answer email from anywhere. The ILO estimates that 22 per cent of the global labor force now works more than 48 hours a week. In the century from 1900 to 2000, average working hours in developed countries fell dramatically, from nearly 3,000 hours a year to under 1,800 – largely due to pressure from the trade-union movement. But in the past decade this trend has begun to reverse. The average working week is creeping upwards in many countries. According to journalist Madeleine Bunting, the number of people in Britain working more than 48 hours has more than doubled since 1998, from 10 per cent to 26 per cent, and one in six workers there clocks more than 60 hours a week.[9] The average working week in Canada is also rising. Two-thirds of workers put in more than 45 hours a week – a 50-per-cent hike over the past 20 years. And despite the buzz about telecommuting and working at home, employers are actually more rigid. Flexitime work arrangements dropped by a third from 2002 to 2012. Leisure time has also plummeted, while just 23 per cent of working Canadians are highly satisfied with life – half as many as in 1991.[10]

It wasn't supposed to be like this. John Maynard Keynes himself once mused that his grandchildren would have the luxury of living in a society where people worked only 15 hours a week. In his 1930 essay, *Economic Possibilities for our Grandchildren,* he wrote: 'We shall endeavor to spread the bread thin on the butter – to make what work there is still to be done to be as widely shared as possible. Three-hour shifts or a 15-hour week may put off the problem for a great while.' Within a hundred years, Keynes predicted, the 'economic problem' would be solved. The standard of living in 'progressive countries' would be between four and eight times higher. And he added: 'In our own lifetimes... we may be able to perform all the operations of agriculture, mining, and manufacture with a quarter of the human effort to which we have been accustomed.'

The promise of labor-saving technology was to release workers from drudgery and servitude – which would then allow a blossoming of creativity, arts and culture. The reality is that technological improvements have put more pressure on people and on the planet. In our current economic model, advances in technology make it possible to produce more goods with less labor. That makes products cheaper so consumers have more disposable income to spend on more stuff. But since fewer workers are needed in the production process, unemployment is the result. In order to keep people working or to boost the number of jobs, economic growth must increase, production must increase and consumption must increase. Growth becomes an endless cycle: efficiency destroys jobs, GDP growth creates them. This might be a trade-off worth making if the capacity of the earth to absorb our waste and provide us with new resources was limitless. But, as we've seen in previous chapters, this is no longer the case. We have run out of room.

There are alternative ways of distributing the benefits of efficiency that could put the brakes on growth and build social capital. At the moment the flipside of increased productivity is increased unemployment – we desperately need growth to create jobs for new and displaced workers. But why not redistribute efficiency savings? If work and wages were shared more equitably, the need for growth to provide new jobs would not be so urgent. More people would work fewer hours but still earn a reasonable income. The social and environmental benefits could be considerable.

Like Galbraith, the French philosopher and radical thinker, Andre Gorz, saw technology as a potential force for liberation. In his 1980 book, *Farewell to the Working Class*, Gorz argued that the computer revolution would fundamentally redefine the nature of work to create a new post-industrial world structured along completely different lines. Leisure time would increase and the impact of human production and consumption on the environment would lessen. But Gorz was not naïve. He understood that this 'pathway to paradise' (the title of his next book in 1984) could only emerge through a new 'politics of time' where all could share equally in the benefits of increasing productivity. He stressed the need for 'self-actualization' and the right to 'autonomous production' where ordinary workers would be freed to pursue their own interests. Gorz was a utopian but his ideas did bear some fruit. Trade unions in both France and Germany picked up on many of his main concerns and in the 1980s they began to bargain for a shorter working week as a way of creating more jobs and providing more leisure time for their members.

In February 2000, France adopted a 35-hour

working week with the slogan: 'Work less, live more.'
Though credited with the creation of 350,000 jobs
over the first decade of its operation, the law has been
under attack ever since. The political Right sees it as an
infringement of the individual rights of both employers
and employees. And competition from low-wage zones
beyond France's borders hasn't helped. The pressure of
globalization leads to a continual ratcheting down of
labor standards and wages, in what trade unions call
a 'race to the bottom'. Workers from one country are
played off against workers from another. To remain
'competitive', employers insist on longer hours, often
at the same rate of pay. In July 2004, employees at
car-parts manufacturer Robert Bosch gave up a 35-hour
week in return for a promise that 300 jobs would not
be exported to the Czech Republic. 'Everyone had
come to accept the fatality of it,' Serge Truscello, a
Bosch employee and union leader at the plant, told
Time magazine, 'either they approved it or they lost
their jobs.' That same summer, workers at two Siemens
factories in Germany agreed to increase their working
week from 35 to 40 hours with no extra pay to stop
2,000 jobs from disappearing to Hungary.[11]
  Proponents of a shorter working week point to

Average annual work time in hours (2011)

Korea	2,193	Ireland	1,664
Greece	2,109	United Kingdom	1,647
Chile	2,068	France	1,554
Italy	1,778	Germany	1,419
United States	1,778	Norway	1,414
Canada	1,702	Netherlands	1,379
Australia	1,686		

Source: OECD (2012), Average annual working time, *Employment
and Labour Markets: Key Tables from OECD*, No. 8

the potential benefits. With more free time, people would have scope to take up hobbies, to exercise, to read and study, to enjoy family life and participate in community activities. Sharing work could also reduce unemployment and, consequently, poverty. But the 'over-employed' would benefit too: as working hours decreased, so would stress, stress-related illnesses and the costs of treating those illnesses. Studies show that people who work long hours in high-energy, fast-paced jobs are more prone to anxiety, depression and other mental-health concerns. The introduction of shorter hours would also have an immediate impact on the environment. Research by the Washington-based Center for Economic and Policy Research found a direct link between environmental footprint and the number of hours worked per year. The study showed that if Americans worked the same number of hours as Europeans (a reduction of about 300 hours a year) their carbon output would drop by 20-30 per cent. In another case, when the US state of Utah mandated a four-day working week for state employees after the 2008 recession, carbon emissions fell by 4,535 tonnes a year. At the same time public vehicles were driven three million fewer miles, which cut fuel consumption by 744,000 gallons and saved $1.4 million.[12]

Other countries have also taken up the torch for reduced work hours. The Netherlands now has the shortest working week in Europe. In the early 1980s, Dutch trade unions shifted gears, trading pay increases for less work. Public-sector unions took the lead – in the early 1990s they began hiring new staff on 80-per-cent contracts. Today, job-sharing is widespread, especially in health and education. Nearly a third of all Dutch citizens work part-time, though the figure is higher for women than men. Sixty per cent of working women had part-time employment in 2001; that number has since risen to 75 per cent. A third of Dutch men either work part-time or squeeze the same hours into fewer days. Reduced working hours are supported by Holland's generous social programs, which allow one (combined) full-time income to support a family. The rise of the four-day week has led to a new phrase – *'Papadag'* or 'Daddy day', when working fathers take a day off to be with their kids. Dutch MP and former news anchor Pia Dijkstra says: 'Our part-time experience has taught us that you can organize work in a rhythm other than nine-to-five. The next generation is turning our part-time culture from a weakness into a strength.'[13]

The Canadian economist Peter A Victor has confirmed that 'spreading employment among more of the labor force' could increase jobs. In his ground-breaking 2008 study, *Managing Without Growth*, Victor built a computer model of what might happen if Canada were to abandon economic growth, aiming for a 'steady state' bounded by strict environmental limits. Victor found that, with major policy changes in key areas, a no-growth economy could increase employment, lower poverty, reduce emissions of greenhouse gases and rein in government debt. Reduced working hours was key to this. 'If more people worked fewer hours, it should be possible to have full employment without relying so much on economic growth,' he wrote. His model for the Canadian economy showed that, 'assuming that labor productivity continues to rise modestly, a reduction in the average work year of around 15 per cent by 2035, to 1,500 hours, would secure full employment.'[14]

Britain's New Economic Foundation (NEF) also suggests that shorter working hours would usher in a better 'work-life balance'. The group's 2010 report, *21 Hours*, argues that a working week of just 21 hours could help reshape modern life, providing at least part of the answer to 'overwork, unemployment, over-consumption, high carbon emissions, low well-being, entrenched inequalities and the lack of time to live sustainably'. The report's co-author, Anna Coote, adds that rewiring the work day would help tackle the rampant consumerism that threatens the planet. 'So many of us live to work, work to earn, and earn to consume,' Coote writes. 'Spending less time in paid work could help us to break this pattern. We'd have more time to be better parents, better citizens, better carers and better neighbors. And we could even become better employees: less stressed, more in control, happier in our jobs and more productive.'[15] The NEF report underlines the environmental benefits of sharing paid work. A less fraught, slower pace would cut down on energy use and reduce carbon emissions. And because shared work would inevitably lead to more equal incomes, the health and social problems associated with inequality could eventually subside. NEF quotes from the Whitehall Studies, a series of surveys of the health of British civil servants which began in 1967 and continue today. The data show that both health and life expectancy are strongly influenced by a combination of stress and lack of control over work. 'People in jobs characterized by low control had higher rates of sickness absence, of mental illness, of heart disease and pain in the lower back.' And here's another thought: perhaps a more equal society would puncture personal anxieties and lessen the intense striving to consume more so as to demonstrate one's social worth.

The need to change direction

Of course, none of this will be a walk in the park. Any attempt to challenge the structure of working life lands us squarely in the wheelhouse of capitalism, where control over the labor process has always been contentious. Workers, pinched by rising costs, debt and job insecurity, are looking to hold on to work, not shed it. Business, too, will need some arm-twisting. Ever since Frederick Taylor launched the concept of 'scientific management' in the early 20th century, employers have jealously guarded their right to dictate the content and flow of work, since both are essential to managing costs and, more critically, producing profits. Although trade unions have battled to wrest control away from managers and owners, progress has been piecemeal. As JM Keynes knew, profit and a certain amount of unemployment go hand in hand. Cutting costs by replacing labor with technology is seen by employers as their prerogative. And the unemployed

Degrowth in action 1

Workers of the world – relax

We have come to see a 35-hour work week not only as normal but also as essential for a thriving society. But the Commissioner for Health with the UK Sustainable Development Commission begs to differ. Anna Coote argues that long work hours are linked to extreme gaps in wealth, environmental degradation, climate change and lots more.

As co-author of the New Economics Foundation report *21 Hours*, Coote proposes that a 21-hour working week should be the norm. It boils down to what we consider 'work': what labor we think is worth paying for. For example, if all the time spent in Britain on unpaid labor – raising children, cooking, household chores and so on – were paid at the minimum wage, it would account for 21 per cent of the country's GDP. 'Informal carers' who attend to the sick and the elderly without pay already 'save' the British economy $125 million a year.

Halving the normal working week could help slash unemployment while reducing state benefits and other social costs. Providing more free time to workers would create space in their lives to exercise, play, sleep and – put simply – enjoy life. Studies consistently show that more leisure means more productivity to boot. Health costs from stress-related illness – one of the greatest burdens on developed nations – would plummet. And gender norms could even improve: men could take on more of what is considered 'women's work' – and fathers could spend increased time with their children.

Reducing unemployment and giving the overworked more free time makes intuitive sense. But on a global scale the math becomes truly interesting: reducing working hours could be one of the keys to solving climate change. On a country-by-country basis there is a direct correlation between the average number of working hours and per-capita greenhouse gas emissions

Frequently employees are extremely hostile – at first. 'Families are on a treadmill of consumerism that is hard to get off,' says Andrew Jackson, of the Canadian Labour Congress. 'But we have found that once people have themselves can be used as a weapon to suppress the wages of those with jobs. It's hard to imagine private corporations ceding this control without major strictures on the use of investment capital, coupled with some kind of broad social contract.

The irony is that, while governments continue to tout economic growth as the route out of recession, in reality they have more or less abandoned the post-War goal of full employment. Mainstream economists now

---

moved to shorter work weeks, they are reluctant to go back – they start to live their lives in a different way.'

Rather than see gains in material efficiency translate into higher consumption (or mass unemployment), we could use technological innovations and increases in efficiency to liberate us from labor.

This makes sense to John de Graaf, founder of the Take Back Your Time coalition. 'Our surveys consistently show that people are most dissatisfied with two things in their lives: time and financial security – not stuff,' he says.

The US coalition advocates that people reduce their working hours voluntarily. 'We have no laws regarding paid vacations and about half the workforce took less than one paid week off last year,' de Graaf says. He believes that the recession, combined with the ecological crisis and widespread unhappiness in wealthy countries – the subject of his film *Affluenza* – could lead to a dramatic paradigm shift in how we think about work.

For many of us, 'work' is inseparable from our sense of self-worth. Yet, says de Graaf, 'a lot of who we are has more to do with how we feel our talents contribute to our community and how valued we feel, rather than our ability to make lots of money.'

Wresting back a bit of control over both would go a long way. 'This not about slacking – this is about balance,' stresses de Graaf.

More time outdoors, more time to play musical instruments and rediscover our creativity, more time with our kids, fitter bodies, reading more, cleaner air, less worrying about the fate of the planet – what's not to like? Throw in less disparity between the rich and the poor, a more affordable standard of living and less corporate control over our time and we approach what some might be tempted to label utopia.

But how to achieve such a society?

'That is the million-dollar question,' says de Graaf. 'Other than educating people that this is about balance, nobody really has the answer yet. It will boil down to making the choice: time versus stuff.' ■

*Adapted from an article by **Zoe Cormier** in* New Internationalist, *434, Jul/Aug 2010.*

claim that an 'official' seven-per-cent unemployment rate is an acceptable figure for 'full employment'. But even this is pretence: folding in the hidden jobless and the underemployed would inflate that number by a factor of three. Meanwhile, industrialized nations continue to pick away at the social safety net woven since the end of the Second World War. Rigid austerity policies target welfare, employment benefits, job security, pensions and healthcare. The British medical journal, *The Lancet*, notes that recent cuts to healthcare in Greece, Spain and Portugal have boosted 'suicides and infectious diseases' and led to 'widespread drug shortages'.[16] For their part, corporations have no interest in hiring more workers, or sweetening the pot for existing workers, unless it's in their direct financial interest. In most cases they are fighting tooth and nail to suppress wages, slash benefits and pare jobs.

All this leaves us in a bind. If we want to fashion a truly sustainable world where humanity lives within Earth's natural limits the route is clear. We need to change direction – quickly. But to do that we are going to have to accept a much more radical approach. Even standard Keynesian prescriptions will not do the trick since, at the end of the day, the purpose of government stimulus is the same – to boost economic growth by expanding demand. And that is the source of our problem, not the solution.

Speaking of solutions, it's now time to turn our thoughts in that direction. We've seen clearly through the previous chapters that the arithmetic of growth no longer adds up. The accomplishments of humankind over the past 200 years have been nothing short of miraculous. And the Enlightenment ideal of unlimited progress, unconstrained by physical boundaries, has served us well, dramatically improving living standards and life expectancy around the world.

But these advancements have not been distributed

equally. Millions of people scrape by on a few dollars a day. Hunger and malnutrition are widespread. Poor sanitation and improper hygiene are still major killers. That is both a tragedy and a deep injustice. And it is especially stark since we have now run out of room. The logic of our old growth-dependent economic system no longer makes sense in a world of ballooning ecological debt and dwindling biodiversity. In the next chapter we'll look at where we go from here.

1 Emily Jane Fox, 'Black Friday shopping hits a new record', nin.tl/1ctyBvS 2 John Kenneth Galbraith, *The Affluent Society*, (40th anniversary edition), Houghton Mifflin, 1998. 3 'Childhood Obesity', US Department of Health, nin.tl/18m2Owb 4 nin.tl/1ctz8hl 5 Jerry Mander, 'Privatization of consciousness', *Monthly Review*, Oct 2012. 6 Eric Slivka 'Apple Hit with Planned Obsolescence Lawsuit in Brazil over Fourth-Generation iPad', 21 Feb 2013, macrumors.com 7 'Debt loads remain at record 165% Canadian per capita', *CBC News*, 15 Mar 2013. 8 'Global Employment Trends 2013', International Labour Organization. 9 Audrey Gillan, 'Work until you drop: how the long-hours culture is killing us', *The Guardian*, 20 Aug 2005. 10 Josh O'Kane, 'Canada's work-life balance more off-kilter than ever', *Globe and Mail*, 25 Oct 2012. 11 Charles P Wallace, 'Not Working', *Time Magazine*, 25 Jul 2004. 12 Zoe Cormier, 'Workers of the world, relax', *New Internationalist* 434, Jul/Aug 2010. 13 Katrin Bennhold, 'Working (Part-Time) in the 21st Century', *New York Times*, 29 Dec 2010. 14 Peter A Victor, *Managing Without Growth*, Edward Elgar, 2008, and 'Questioning Economic Growth', *Nature*, Vol 468, 18 Nov 2010. 15 'Shorter working week soon inevitable, forecasts nef', 13 Feb 2010, neweconomics.org 16 'Financial crisis, austerity, and health in Europe', Marina Karanikolos et al, *The Lancet*, Vol 381, No 9874, 13 April 2013.

8 On the road to degrowth

The austerity programs of the present represent the death throes of the old growth-chasing model. The interest now is less in sustainability, an idea largely hijacked by big business, than in *décroissance* or degrowth, with initiatives inspired by this beginning to flower all over the world. Renewing our cultures and economies will involve re-evaluating all our assumptions and practices – but there really is no alternative.

'If I have seen further it is only by standing on the shoulders of giants.'

Isaac Newton

The great English mathematician, physicist and philosopher Isaac Newton was not a historian but he understood the past. We stand on the shoulders of giants, as he wrote. The world we know today owes much to those who have come before us. The dizzying advances in science, technology and engineering that we've witnessed over the past century have dramatically altered the shape and nature of human affairs. We no longer inhabit the world of our parents or our grandparents. The tools we use to communicate have morphed from quill pens to smartphones; our modes of travel have shifted from horseback to jet planes and private automobiles. The kind of work we do; whether we have enough to eat; how long we live; how healthy and comfortable are our lives; how we spend our leisure time; how we relate to our friends, family and community; the integrity of the natural world: all these aspects of life and many more have changed in profound and surprising ways. We are globalized and interconnected; yet we are riven by growing economic inequality and environmental calamity. We do not often stop to think about the depth of this monumental shift and what it implies for our collective human future.

There are few politicians, business leaders or intellectuals who have the courage or the leadership skills to challenge old orthodoxies. We stand on the shoulders of giants. But we rarely look down or ask how we got so far, so fast.

Some things are self-evident. We have created an economic system that is producing vast wealth for the few at the expense of the majority. The model is broken and the damage to people, communities and the natural world is accelerating. In the aftermath of the great financial meltdown of 2008 and the continuing instability of the global economy, there is urgent need – and a deep yearning – for balance and equity. The search for alternatives has never been more urgent. We face a calamitous future unless we as a global community can work out a gradual, peaceful transition to a new economic model.

At the moment we are offered two options to escape our economic paralysis, both firmly within the old paradigm. The first path is stimulus spending, the traditional Keynesian remedy of boosting demand by increasing government spending and, consequently, public debt. Keynesians argue that if the economy is collapsing and private investors are unwilling to invest because of 'uncertainties' in the market then governments have an obligation to intervene to save the system from itself. The main focus should be employment and social stability. Debt is merely a short-term problem that will disappear once growth resumes. Government coffers will fill as taxes pour into a revived economy. We saw this remedy in full force in the immediate aftermath of the 2008 crisis when governments around the globe pumped billions into new spending. The G20 nations alone earmarked more than $2 trillion – about 1.4 per cent of global GDP. Amounts ranged from 1.5 per cent of GDP in Britain to 6 per cent in the US to over 12 per cent of GDP in China. Stimulus spending put money in people's pockets by cranking up social-welfare support and by creating jobs. The global economy was spinning wildly out of control until governments moved to avert a crash.

But once in the clear it wasn't long before old habits reappeared and the 'deficit hawks' began to circle, fretting over 'unsustainable' government debt. Those responsible for the economic chaos – the big banks, mortgage dealers and finance titans whose reckless pursuit of double-digit returns inflated the real-estate bubble – were bailed out by public funds. Yet now they were calling the shots. Finance ministers, in thrall to this business élite, did an about face and zeroed in on government debt as the real roadblock to recovery. The theory was that investors would not get back into the growth game without a guarantee of stability and that meant one thing – balanced budgets and reduced debt. The common-sense parallel, often cited, was that governments are like households and that you can't spend more than you can earn without getting into trouble. Consequently, the way to reduce debt and rebuild market confidence was austerity, not stimulus. This policy of 'tough love' is now being played out across Europe, Britain and Canada, with Australia's new right-wing government also likely to sign on. And it is also the 'big stick' that Republicans in Washington wield to beat back attempts by the Obama administration to boost federal spending. Instead of providing stimulus, governments now aim to slash public spending and shrink the state.

The austerity dead end

These concerns dominate economic policy in G20 nations and across the OECD, even though there is zero proof that austerity leads to growth. Just the opposite: it appears both harsh and ineffective medicine, disturbingly similar to the 19th-century practice of bleeding a patient to cure disease. Liberal analysts like Nobel Prize-winning economist Paul Krugman have been hammering away at the austerity agenda for years, not only because it doesn't work but also because it creates a lot of collateral damage in the process. In Europe, where austerity is in vogue, growth has completely stalled. The annual inflation rate in the Euro zone now hovers around one per cent while unemployment remains scandalously high. According to Krugman, long-term unemployment is now a permanent, 'corrosive' feature in most Western economies and austerity is only making things worse. You can't understand austerity, he says, without talking about class and inequality. 'The austerity agenda looks a lot like a simple expression of upper-class preferences, wrapped in a façade of academic rigor. What the top one per cent wants becomes what economic science says we must do.'[1]

Hard truths: across the EU nearly 27 million people are jobless. In Greece, Spain and Portugal unemployment is the highest it's been since the Great Depression. Youth unemployment is at record levels: more than 60 per cent of young people in Greece and 56 per cent in Spain are unemployed with no signs of improvement. There is talk of a 'lost generation' in Spain and Greece. Thousands of young people are simply voting with their feet. The National Statistics Institute reports that 365,000 Spaniards between 16 and 29 left the country in the first three months of 2012.

Like the disastrous structural-adjustment programs imposed on dozens of developing nations in the 1980s and early 1990s, austerity is an attack on the poor in the name of debt repayment and economic restructuring. The prescription is similar: a reduced role for the state; privatization of public assets; labor-market 'flexibility' (a code word meaning reduced standards, benefits and protection for workers); a loosening of environmental regulations; and reduced spending on education, healthcare and social welfare. But, unlike the 1980s, it is not the IMF and the World Bank twisting the arms of distant developing nations. Today it's the so-called *troika* pulling the strings. The IMF is still involved. But the group imposing structural adjustment also includes the European Union and the European Central Bank.

New research underlines the notion that social ills are rooted in inequality. Widening income gaps weaken society and make things worse for everyone, not just the poor. As mentioned in the last chapter, in their book, *The Spirit Level*, epidemiologists Richard Wilkinson and Kate Pickett compared data on health and social development across 23 countries and found that citizens in more equal societies almost always come out ahead.[2]

Equality is good for us. It fosters stronger, healthier, more democratic societies and helps build community. Yet inequality is growing almost everywhere and those in power refuse to do anything about it. All hope is placed in economic growth as the safety valve: inequality is excused as the price you pay for a dynamic system where everyone has the chance to be rich. Life is a gamble but you could be a winner! This is the prevailing myth that enables the system to keep going. Against reason, science and empirical evidence, the old orthodoxy holds firm. The 'invisible hand' of the market will sort things out. *Laissez-faire* is best. Economic growth will be our salvation, providing jobs and prosperity. Technology will save us.

Yet people feel there is something wrong, even if they can't quite identify the problem. Middle-class budgets are stretched while the number of billionaires grows. Young people can't find decent jobs or affordable housing; the gap between the one per cent and the rest of us is widening; social services are pared back while the welfare state is dismantled. In the US, where belief in the free market reigns supreme, the top one per cent saw income growth of 58 per cent between 1993 and 2010 while the income of everyone else rose by just 6.4 per cent. People have lost faith in big government, big banks, big business, Wall Street and the City of London. Describing the wrenching social upheaval of his time, Karl Marx wrote: 'all that is solid melts into air'.[3] This feeling of unease is rampant today.

The simple fact is that an economic and political system which does not deliver for the majority will not be sustainable in the long run. Cracks will inevitably appear. As we've seen in popular uprisings from the Arab Spring to the Occupy Movement to the anti-austerity demonstrations that exploded across Europe in 2012, eventually people lose faith in the *status quo* when it fails to deliver. The legitimacy of existing institutions and arrangements is challenged.

We know the market system does not operate smoothly. Periods of boom and bust are endemic, even predictable. Sometimes there is a mild downturn in the normal 'business cycle'; on other occasions there are more serious disruptions, a full-blown recession – or worse. Slow growth or no growth is a sign of failure. That's why, in the larger scheme of things, choosing between austerity and stimulus is a mug's game.

Neither path will take us to where we need to go. Sustainability is the goal. But what does the word really mean and how do we get there?

The emergence of sustainability as an idea

The concept of 'sustainability' first emerged three decades ago with the publication of *Our Common Future*, a 1987 report from the UN World Commission on Environment and Development, chaired by Norwegian prime minister Gro Harlem Brundtland. It became popularly known as the Brundtland Report and broke new ground, raising fundamental questions about the link between poverty, resource consumption and environmental decline. 'Poverty is a major cause and effect of global environmental problems,' the Report noted. 'It is therefore futile to attempt to deal with environmental problems without a broader perspective that encompasses the factors underlying world poverty and international inequality.'[4]

The Brundtland Report captured public and media attention with its emphasis on 'sustainable development', which it defined in a much-quoted phrase as 'development that meets the needs of the present without compromising the ability of future generations to meet their own needs'. *Our Common Future* stands the test of time surprisingly well, especially in its analysis of the see-saw relationship between environmental decline and global prosperity. The Report's highlighting of the 'accelerating ecological interdependence among nations' was also prescient. 'Ecology and economy are becoming ever more interwoven locally, regionally, nationally, and globally into a seamless net of causes and effects,' the document noted. The Report's description of the symptoms of ecological stress is also eerily familiar: deforestation, urbanization, the loss of biodiversity, desertification, toxic waste, air and water pollution, groundwater depletion, even global warming, are all featured.

The heart of the problem, the Brundtland Report argued, was the nefarious tag team of global poverty and inequality. 'Developing countries must operate in a world in which the resources gap between most developing and industrial nations is widening; in which the industrial world dominates in the rule-making of some key international bodies; and in which the industrial world has already used much of the planet's ecological capital. This *inequality* is the planet's main "environmental" problem; it is also its main "development" problem… A world in which *poverty* is endemic will always be prone to ecological and other catastrophes.'

With that unswerving focus on social and economic justice, the document was a radical wake-up call. But in other ways the Brundtland Report was a product of its time, its core analysis firmly anchored in technological hubris and the notion that environmental limits could be managed by a combination of human ingenuity and common sense.

Our Common Future was relentlessly optimistic, predicting a 'new era of economic growth... based on policies that sustain and expand the environmental resource base'. There were no absolute limits the Report stated flatly, only 'limitations imposed by the present state of technology and social organization on environmental resources and by the ability of the biosphere to absorb the effects of human activities.' But technology and social organization can be 'managed and improved to make way for a new era of economic growth'.

Today, gazing out from the shoulders of giants, we know more. 'Managed growth' is no longer an option in a world bounded by absolute limits. To reach true sustainability we need to ask *not how to restart the growth machine, but how to live without it*. How can we construct a new economic model that meets our basic human needs without roasting the planet, exhausting our finite natural resources and jeopardizing the essential natural systems that support life on Earth?

The notion of boundless growth is so ingrained in our collective psyche that a *non-growing* economy is beyond comprehension for most people – the deluded chatter of eggheads and tree huggers. Yet the idea has appeared throughout the history of economic thought. More than two centuries ago, John Stuart Mill in his massive *Principles of Political Economy* embraced this notion and called it 'the stationary state'. Countering the claim that zero growth would translate into stagnation, poverty and unemployment, Mill argued that 'a stationary condition of capital and population implies no stationary state of human improvement'. Instead, he stressed, 'there would be as much scope as ever for all kinds of mental culture, and moral and social progress; as much room for improving the Art of Living and much more likelihood of its being improved, when minds cease to be engrossed by the art of getting on.'

We need to turn the old orthodoxy on its head. Luckily, a framework for building a new economy is emerging. Today no-growth advocates use the term 'steady state' rather than Mill's phrase 'stationary state'. Others claim zero growth is not enough. We must go even further and pursue 'degrowth' – not just flat lining but a systematic rewinding of growth in those countries where the costs already exceed the benefits. Degrowth advocates don't suggest going back to the 19th century but they do stress the need for rich countries to scale back both industrial production and material expectations *to clear the ecological space for*

Degrowth in action 2

Vive la décroissance!

Serge Latouche looks the part – a 70-something former professor from the Université de Paris Sud. But he doesn't sound like one. The grizzled economist is the force behind the French 'degrowth' movement and one of Europe's leading critics of economic growth and consumerism.

Latouche believes 'growth' is a term that obscures more than it reveals. 'If you take into account damage to the environment and public health, the results are usually negative. Yet when we measure gross domestic product (GDP), the pollution, diseases and deaths it causes are added to the plus side.'

Latouche was a late convert to the anti-growth camp. It wasn't until 2001 that he spoke for the first time of 'degrowth' – at a UNESCO conference in Paris, linking his critique of development to economic growth. He called for selective economic contraction to stop environmental decay, using the French word – *décroissance*.

'The English translation, "degrowth", pleased most of the audience, so I stuck with it,' Latouche recalls. 'But I would rather speak of "a-growth", much like we speak of "a-theism". Degrowth is only a catchword.'

Maybe – but in the years since the UNESCO conference, degrowth has become a hot idea in France. Even former French president Nicolas Sarkozy got the bug, asking Nobel-Prize-winning economists Joseph Stiglitz and Amartya Sen in 2008 to look into new ways of measuring prosperity without relying on GDP. The report was released as 'The Commission on the Measurement of Economic Performance and Social Progress'.

Two magazines, *La Décroissance* and *Entropia*, also spread the degrowth gospel in the country. And journalists like *Le Monde Dipomatique*'s Hervé Kempf endorse the idea. Several farmer and consumer organizations rally *those who need it.* They base their logic on simple mathematics and global justice. We cannot, in good conscience, continue on our current path of over-development while two-thirds of the world's population, mostly in the Global South, still lives at or below the poverty level. The poor majority has a moral claim to its rightful share of the Earth's resources. They urgently require economic growth – a living wage, housing, schools, hospitals, and basic infrastructure for sanitation and clean water – while we in the rich world must redefine what we mean by the good life. As ecological footprint data shows, we are already in a

---

behind the movement – from the French association for organic agriculture to 'locavores' – people who want to eat seasonal food from their own region.

But Latouche's influence goes beyond France's borders. In Italy, the monthly magazine *Carta* spreads his critique of development and economic growth. And the 'slow food' movement is also on the same page. In Spain, several university professors teach courses in degrowth. In the run-up to the December 2009 UN Climate Change Conference in Copenhagen, activists and grassroots environment networks formed Climate Justice Action (CJA), which aims to take 'the urgent actions needed to avoid catastrophic climate change', including embracing degrowth as an alternative. There have also been numerous international conferences on degrowth – Paris in 2008, Barcelona in 2010, Montreal and Venice in 2012. And degrowth is a strong current in the growing 'transition towns' movement.

Latouche believes that facts on the ground will turn the tide: 'The climate catastrophe has spawned wars for oil, for water and gold. We have more pandemics and a massive loss of species that are essential to environmental equilibrium.'

But it's not a slam dunk.

Despite Sarkozy's blue-ribbon panel on GDP, the number of working hours in France has been slowly increasing since 1997. Like the rest of Europe, the country sees growth as the only way to fight unemployment. So how to make Latouche's vision a reality?

'We have to change our values. We need to replace egoism with altruism, competition with co-operation and obsessive performance with leisure. But the problem is that values are systemic – they are both cause and effect. Without a radical questioning of the system, the value change will remain limited.' ∎

*Adapted from an article by **Julio Godoy** in* New Internationalist *434, Jul/Aug 2010.*

condition of 'overshoot', living beyond the carrying capacity of the planet, undercutting the essential ecosystems that support human life and biodiversity. With a global population of more than seven billion we consume the equivalent of 1.5 Earths. According to the Global Footprint Network, it takes the Earth 18 months to regenerate what we use in one year, a clear sign that we are losing the sustainability race. And with growth as our goal we are destined to fall further and further behind. By the 2030s, as we chew through what's left of our natural capital, we'll need more like two Earths to support us. You can see why degrowth advocates worry about the math.

Yet growth continues apace. As population and consumption expand across Asia, Africa and Latin America, the demand for food, energy and natural resources accelerates. It's clear we are sailing into uncharted seas. The Australian social scientist Ted Trainer argues that a conscious process of 'under-development' of developing nations combined with 'overproduction' and 'overconsumption' in the rich world is a lethal mix. 'Levels of material affluence are far too high to be kept up for long or to spread to all of the world's people,' he writes. 'The magnitude of the overshoot requires enormous reductions that cannot be made within or by consumer-capitalist society.'[5]

The idea that we would deliberately stop or cut back economic growth is unfathomable to most people, especially those in power – politicians, investors, business leaders, media élites – who are heavily invested in the current set-up. Indeed, it may be naïve to assume that those whose welfare and worldview are so directly linked to the current model will stand up and denounce the system. It would be the equivalent of a nuclear engineer suggesting that nuclear power should be scrapped. The belief system is too all-enveloping even to imagine dissent. That is why traditional politicians on the Left or Right are unlikely to provide leadership here. The Enlightenment notion that progress and increased prosperity will emerge from improved technology and the scientific method has been the driving force of the last two centuries. All but the Greens among political tendencies have endorsed this central idea, united in the belief that more is better, that the future is perfectible and that increasing material wealth is both our birthright and our duty. While poverty exists we need growth to fight it: to do otherwise would be amoral. As the pro-growth writer Daniel Ben-Ami has argued: 'as long as we are limited by scarcity we will not be able to flourish as a species.'[6] The baleful irony is that we will neither flourish as a species, nor improve the lives of the poor majority, if we blithely destroy the basis of our future prosperity. Standing still or going backward falls outside the framework of contemporary political thought. Yet for the sake of our collective survival and the health of the

---

Degrowth: what is it?

'Sustainable degrowth is a downscaling of production and consumption that increases human well-being and enhances ecological conditions and equity on the planet. It calls for a future where societies live within their ecological means, with open, localized economies and resources more equally distributed through new forms of democratic institutions. Such societies will no longer have to 'grow or die'. Material accumulation will no longer hold a prime position in the population's cultural imagination.

'The primacy of efficiency will be substituted by a focus on sufficiency, and innovation will no longer focus on technology for technology's sake but will concentrate on new social and technical arrangements that will enable us to live convivially and frugally.

'Degrowth does not only challenge the centrality of GDP as an overarching policy objective but proposes a framework for transformation to a lower and sustainable level of production and consumption, a shrinking of the economic system to leave more space for human co-operation and ecosystems.' ■

From Research & Degrowth / Recherche & Décroissance (degrowth.org), an association of academics and researchers looking to raise public awareness and understanding of the concept of degrowth.

planet it is the only future that makes sense.

But what would a non-growing economy mean in practice? The Centre for the Advancement of the Steady State Economy (CASSE) is one of the key non-governmental organizations attempting to describe what this new economy would be like and how we can make the transition. CASSE is a big tent that brings together under one canvas many of the leading figures who challenge the conventional growth model. There are differences of detail in their analysis but they share one fundamental starting-point described at length in this *No Nonsense Guide*. We have exceeded the biophysical limits of the planet and in much of the world the costs of growth now outweigh the benefits. The result is that we are living on borrowed time, squandering finite natural capital while mortgaging the future. Despite the warning signs – from desertification to deforestation to climate change – we continue confidently down the same path.

According to CASSE, a steady state aims for 'a stable level of resource consumption and a stable population... where energy and resource use are reduced to the levels that are within ecological limits and where the goal of maximizing economic output is replaced by the goal of maximizing the quality of life.'[7]

Quality of life is really the nub of the issue – what Mill elegantly called the 'Art of Living'. Critics suggest that a steady-state economy will lead to joyless regimentation and enforced poverty. But this is a crass diversion. Economic activity will not come screeching to a halt. Instead the goal will be balance and equity, two things in short supply in our growth-oriented system. We will need to aim for a new 'economy of sufficiency' or what some have called a 'solidarity economy' – one based on co-operation rather than competition and defined by ecological limits. In other words an *intentionally* non-growing economy.

In practice this will require a fundamental shift

in values. Instead of mindless accumulation and an unquestioning search for 'more', we will need to look elsewhere for motivation and meaning. US sociologist Juliet Schor describes this important shift in cultural values as a journey towards 'plenitude'. By this, Schor means we need to step back from the 'commodified' relations of the market and think about essential human and community relationships.

What gives life value? How much stuff do we really need?

Saving the planet requires a new set of alternative values. At the very least we will need to reconsider consumerism, jump off the treadmill of globalization and invest in our local communities. This implies more co-operative and democratic ways of organizing society. It calls for interdependence rather than competition and a mix of strategies so as gradually to extract ourselves from the clutches of the unrestricted market. Schor talks about 'time wealth' rather than 'monetary wealth' and supports 'self-provisioning' (growing your own food, making things yourself) and 'true materialism' (using sturdy, durable goods that can be maintained and repaired). More critically, she advocates small-scale 'investments in one another and in our communities' as a way of bolstering self-sufficiency and rebuilding local economies.

Forty years ago EF Schumacher outlined the importance of 'scale' in his book, *Small is Beautiful*. Modern society, he wrote, is transfixed by the 'idolatry of giantism' which is 'incapable' of solving any of our real problems. Our goal is to bring things down to the level of people again, he believed. Prefiguring the growing enthusiasm today for 'localization', he wrote: 'We must learn to think in terms of an articulated structure that can cope with a multiplicity of small-scale units.'[8]

The question of scale is no less critical today to understanding the dilemma of limitless growth in a finite world. In a steady state with zero growth, supply lines for both production and distribution will need to be dramatically shortened and energy inputs minimized. We will need to wean ourselves from our dependency on fossil fuels and depend increasingly on non-polluting sources of renewable energy. The highly centralized, corporate-led, globalized system which emerged over the past half century is built on a foundation of cheap energy from oil, coal and natural gas. Because of the threat to the global climate that era must now draw to a close. In a non-growing economy, this deregulated, privatized, profit-driven system will be recognized for what it is: a colossal barrier to our future well-being; profligate, wasteful and harmful to both people and the environment.

The challenge is to broaden our idea of the good life beyond consumption alone. That does not imply a wholesale rejection of material things. A steady state will continue to produce those things we need. The products of our hands, our minds and our machines are an essential part of what it means to be human. They are coded with symbolical meaning and they reflect our imagination, our intellect and our creativity. A post-growth world needs to value material goods but understand that an addiction to too much 'stuff' is suicidal. An individual's right to consume must take a back seat to the rights of nature and the broader public interest. Ultimately, culture and community matter more and resonate more deeply. Family, friends, faith, music, dance, conversation, theater, love, co-operation and many other human pursuits need to be at the core of what we value most.

But knowing where we must go doesn't make it easy. The transition to a new economic model is not going to happen overnight or without fierce opposition from those who profit from the current set-up. Lip service is paid to the notion of sustainability by even the most rapacious corporations. These days it's simply smart public relations. Companies like BP,

Dow Chemical and Rio Tinto are among the biggest polluters on earth, yet they continue to trumpet their green credentials. BP, for example, publishes a *Sustainability Review* where it outlines its commitment to bringing as much oil and gas as possible into production in the most efficient, least environmentally damaging way. The *Review* describes BP as a keen player in the Alberta tar sands. But it neglects to add that tar-sands mining may be the most destructive resource project on the planet. Even the US Department of Energy says that tar sands are a carbon bomb, producing three times more emissions per barrel and 22 per cent more greenhouse gas than conventional oil.[9] Not to mention the vast expanse of boreal forest that is mowed down, the millions of liters of fresh water consumed or skyrocketing cancer rates in local communities. And then there is BP's rival Shell, which was hauled on to the carpet by the UK Advertising Standards Authority for an ad claiming that its multi-billion-dollar tar sands investment was a contribution to a 'sustainable energy future'.[10] So much for corporate sustainability.

There are few globe-spanning firms that have not wrapped themselves in the flag of 'green growth', proudly displaying their eco credentials in order to get a leg up in the market. Environmentalists call it 'greenwashing'. Everything from hydraulic fracking and open-pit mining to jet travel and ocean fish farming is touted as 'sustainable' as long as the environment is given a cursory tip of the hat.

As a result, the word sustainability has become something of an empty buzzword. The truth is that the efforts of individual corporations to clean up their act are really side issues. Because for sustainability to have real meaning it needs to address the big picture. Just as replacing your old light bulbs with compact fluorescents or driving a hybrid electric car will not stop climate change, 'greening' the production process of one corporation, or even an entire industry, will

Degrowth in action 3

Toss it? No way!

It wasn't so long ago that people fixed things when they broke. Fifty years ago, if you had a hole in the toe of your sock, you (or your mother) mended it. If the washing machine stopped working, you called in the local repairer. In most Western countries this is no longer the case. We live in a throwaway society where a vast amount of perfectly good stuff gets chucked into the garbage with scarcely a second thought.

People no longer have the skills to make simple repairs to household items or they can't be bothered. Or it's easier and almost as cheap to buy a new one. Why repair your toaster when you can get a replacement made in China, Cambodia, Honduras or some other low-wage country?

There's a term for this: planned obsolescence.

Consumer goods are designed with a limited lifespan so that when they break down you will buy more. It's good for economic growth, good for business and good for the market. Unfortunately, it's not so good for the Earth. In fact, it's part of the deadly mix of greed, ignorance and short-sighted economic policies that is driving the planet to the brink.

Martine Postma had a better idea. In October 2009, the former Dutch journalist decided to challenge this pattern of consumer waste and resource depletion. She opened the first Repair Café in Amsterdam, a space where people could gather to share skills and help each other salvage goods that would previously have ended up in the local landfill. It's a way of reinforcing and building collective knowledge where neighbors can swap stories while mending a skirt or tinkering with a broken blender. Volunteer 'fixers' gain the satisfaction of helping others learn while people save money and reduce the amount of junk in the environment.

You could call it sustainability in action – a welcome alternative to our 'toss-it-and-forget-it' mentality. And it's spreading quickly.

With support from the Dutch environment ministry, Martine set up the Repair Café Foundation with the goal of spreading the word to communities across the country. There are now 20 Repair Cafés in the Netherlands and nearly 50 outside Holland – from Berlin and Brighton to Palo Alto and Toronto.

When the first US Repair Café in Palo Alto, California, opened in October 2012, more than 100 people showed up. The Toronto Repair Café was launched in the summer of 2013 with a monthly workshop where 'fixers' repair everything from broken lamps to busted chairs. 'It is a community initiative,' founder Wei Chu Cheng told the *Toronto Star*. 'The fixers teach the visitors how to fix things themselves. They explain to the visitors what they're doing, and at the end of the visit, they'll understand what went wrong and how it was fixed.'

If you think a Repair Café would be a valuable addition to your community, contact repaircafe.org for more information. ∎

not make growth sustainable. In order to turn the behemoth around we need to realize that growth is a political problem that requires a political solution. We can only solve the problem by working collectively.

That's why growth critics call for a multi-pronged approach, working on theory and practice at the same time. A key concept is resilience, the ability to bounce back from stress and crises. The Canadian political scientist Thomas Homer-Dixon believes that our growth economy works to reduce resilience and thus increases the likelihood of social and ecological collapse. Governments, he says, need to become more active in promoting resilience since the private sector sees it essentially as a drain on profits. Today's globalized capitalism, in its most dogmatic form, assumes that 'larger scale, faster growth, less government, and more efficiency, connectivity and speed are always better. Slack is always waste. So resilience – even as an idea, let alone as a goal of public policy – isn't found anywhere on the agendas of our societies' leaders.'[11]

But how do we create a resilient economy? We do it by planning, plugging holes, patching weak spots and constantly challenging the straitjacket of economic growth that constrains us. We may not know exactly how a zero-growth world would function but we do know that our basic assumptions must change. With this in mind, let's look at some of the key policy changes needed to pop the growth genie back in the bottle.

Stabilizing population

'Look after the people and the population will take care of itself.' That was a popular slogan of those who supported a fairer deal for the developing world 30 years ago. The implication is that wealthier, healthier, better educated, well fed and housed people will decide on their own to have fewer children. The intervening decades have borne that out. In general, when living standards improve population rates fall. We see this across the industrialized world. In most rich countries population growth is already at, or below, the natural replacement rate (the point where deaths equal births). For these countries, immigration is the only way to maintain a growing population.

Some 45 years ago *The Population Bomb,* written by biologists Paul and Anne Erlich, became an international – and contentious – best-seller.[12] The book described the links between population growth, resource consumption and environmental decline. The central argument was that the Earth has a finite capacity to provide food, shelter and a decent life for an exponentially growing population pursuing the consumer dream. The book stirred up a hornets' nest. The Erlichs were pilloried by the Left as neo-Malthusians who naively targeted overpopulation as the main problem rather than inequality. And they were attacked by the Right for insinuating that involving the state in individual fertility decisions, rather than market forces, could solve the problem.

Whatever the authors' intentions, their book succeeded in heightening public concern and prompted Western nations to funnel millions of aid dollars into Third World population programs. Fears of swarms of people from the impoverished South trashing the environment, undermining the global economy and enviously eyeing the fleshpots of Europe and America triggered some nasty, coercive interventions in population control. Indira Gandhi's forced sterilization program in India was among the most notorious. The country declared a state of emergency in 1975 and in the same year more than eight million poor villagers – mostly men – were sterilized.

The Population Bomb certainly pulled no punches. There are only two solutions to our dilemma, the Erlichs wrote. 'One is a "birth rate solution" in which we find ways to lower the birth rate. The other is a "death rate solution" in which ways to raise the death rate – war, famine, pestilence – find us.'[12] What seemed gloomily pessimistic at the time sounds less so today. Demographers see the global population peaking at around nine billion by 2050. That's a threefold hike since 1950 when there were scarcely three billion of us on the planet. Most of these new citizens will live in the exploding urban areas of Asia and Africa where living conditions are difficult and basic infrastructure stretched.

Yet the world has changed dramatically in the last three decades. On the one hand, most countries now have family-planning programs in place and birth rates continue to drop globally. On the other hand, deregulated investment, coupled with wide-open markets, has spiked economic growth across much of the Global South, especially in India and China, where millions have improved living standards and aspire to live like middle-class Westerners. This 'aspiration bomb' is, of course, not confined to those two economic powerhouses. The same yearnings are spread across the developing world, wherever the hope of a better life glimmers.

How the extra two billion people on the planet will live depends on the delicate interplay between resource use and population numbers. The fundamental tension raised in *The Population Bomb* remains. Without redistribution of wealth and income, an expanding population requires more economic growth if per-capita GDP is not to decline. There is no appetite for tackling these fundamental issues among the world's political élites. The old paradigm is still firmly in place.

From a no-growth perspective, a stable population is essential. More people use more resources, produce more waste and have a proportionately bigger impact on the environment. We need to stabilize per-capita resource use but we also need to hold the line on population. It's not one or the other, but both. As the summary report from the first Steady State Economy

Conference notes: 'we need smaller footprints but we also need fewer feet.'[13]

Those two billion new arrivals cannot live at the same level of excessive consumption as the average European or North American. Yet justice and equity demands that basic living standards and material prosperity are shared across the planet. This is not possible unless rich countries voluntarily suspend or reduce growth so those who still need it can pursue it.

Controlling human fertility by edict has never worked. Population will level off when wealth is distributed more equally. That's well known. But increased living standards are not the only factor reducing births. When women win the right to education and employment; when healthcare improves and infant mortality rates drop; when women have the power to control their fertility through contraception and abortion: all of these trends cause birth rates to fall.

Reducing inequality

Inequality is the root of many health problems and social pathologies which have steep human and economic costs. To avoid class conflict and promote social harmony, a zero-growth world must aim to be radically egalitarian since we can no longer look to economic growth as the ultimate solution to poverty. Both wealth and income will need to be more fairly distributed.

Effective progressive taxation will require both corporations and rich individuals to pay their rightful share. Companies will no longer be able to avoid taxes by stashing profits in Luxembourg or the Cayman Islands. Among the cases in point: the Bank of America had offshore profits of $17.2 billion in 2012 and paid no US taxes,[14] while other wealthy companies like Apple, Amazon and Facebook avoid taxes by transferring profits to subsidiaries in low tax zones. According to a US Congress investigation in 2011, more than 60 per cent of Apple's $34 billion in profits were redirected to companies registered in Ireland, where the corporate tax rate is a paltry two per cent.

Inequality is about more than money; it's also about power. Institutional structures backed by business interests and political élites block change because they benefit directly from the *status quo*. That's why public policy often differs from public opinion. One way to address this is to expand those institutions that are inherently more democratic and not led by the profit motive. As corporate critic Marjorie Kelly notes: 'Our politics and economy are so intertwined that imbalances in wealth and ownership have eroded our political democracy. To fix this, we need to democratize the economic aspect of sovereignty.'[15] The public sector deserves more respect. So do non-profit groups, credit unions and small businesses for whom growth is not the fundamental *raison d'être*.

But perhaps the co-operative movement is the best bet for advancing equality. Co-operatives offer a way to democratize ownership and to counter the divisions and inequalities of the market economy. The co-op model is a challenge to the hyper-competitive, winner-take-all mold of corporate capitalism. Co-operatives show there is an alternative to the market where profit is not the sole objective and where, theoretically, fairness is institutionalized and people are at the center of decision-making.

There is no question that mutual support works. The massive Mondragon Co-operative, a $24-billion global operation in Spain's Basque region, is a case in point. Of the group's 270 component companies, only one went out of business after the crisis of 2008. And all these workers were absorbed by other co-ops.

Environmental justice means tackling inequality. Only by redistribution can we hope to slow the rate of growth. But what about the Global South, where average incomes are a tiny fraction of those in the North and where traditional economic growth still increases welfare when reasonably distributed? Rich countries will need to reduce growth to free up resources and provide ecological space for the poor. But poor countries will also need financial and technological support from the rich to make sure their growth remains within the biophysical limits of

Degrowth in action 4

The co-operative solution

According to the International Co-operative Association, more than a billion people are now involved in co-operative ventures – as members, customers, employees or worker/owners. Co-operatives also provide over 100 million jobs – 20 per cent more than transnational corporations.

There are producer, retail and consumer co-ops and they're spread across every industry. Members may benefit from cheaper prices, friendly service or better access to markets but, most importantly, the democratic structure of co-operatives means members are ultimately in charge. A core principle is 'one member, one vote'. It's that sense of control that builds social capital and makes co-operatives such a vital source of community identity. Profits might be reinvested in the business, shared among members or channeled to the local community.

Can co-ops 'crowd out' capitalism? Probably not. But they can at least prepare the ground and help to expand democratic space. University of Wisconsin sociologist Erik Olin Wright believes they can play a vital role in rebuilding the public sphere and creating a wedge between the market and the state. Wright talks of a 'symbiotic' transformation where co-ops spearhead a wider democratic surge to help bolster civil society and put down roots 'in the cracks of the existing system'.[16] Co-operatives can point the way towards a different kind of economic model where people control capital and not the other way around.

Because they exist to benefit their members, rather than to line the pockets of private shareholders, co-operatives are fundamentally more democratic. They empower people. They build community. And they strengthen local economies. ∎

Facts on Co-ops

- More than a billion members worldwide
- Provide 100 million jobs
- Produce half the global agricultural output
- Finance co-ops serve more than 857 million people
- Top 300 co-ops generate $1.6 trillion a year

Source: International Co-operative Alliance

the earth. Co-operation is paramount. Going it alone will no longer work when the environmental concerns are global.

Reining in resource use

This topic was discussed in detail in Chapter 2 so we'll summarize here. Our use of natural resources over the past century has increased exponentially in lockstep with growth. The expanding human economy has altered nature fundamentally and threatens to undermine the ecosystem services on which all life depends. All material inputs into the economic process must be returned to the environment as waste. We are producing millions of tons of toxic pollutants so quickly that the Earth is incapable of absorbing or recycling them. Some of these emissions, like CO_2, are key drivers in destabilizing the global climate. We need to recognize that the economy is a subset of the environment, not the other way around.

The eminent ecological economist Herman Daly suggests three basic rules to define the 'material throughput' of a zero-growth economy:

1 Renewable resources should be harvested at rates that don't exceed regeneration rates.
2 The rate of depletion of non-renewable resources should not exceed the rate of creation of non-renewable substitutes.
3 Pollutants should not be released at a rate that exceeds the natural capacity of the environment to recycle or absorb them.

Contracting and converging

How can we control both resource use and damaging emissions so as to reduce wear and tear on the planet? The challenge is to establish limits or caps on what can be taken out of the environment and what can be dumped back. Ecological tax reform would shift the tax burden from economic 'goods' (incomes) to environmental 'bads' (pollution). Eventually this would raise resource prices and encourage reduced, more efficient resource use.

Letting the market determine damaging green-house-gas emissions through a 'cap-and-trade scheme' is a dead end, another way for corporations to make money rather than deal with the issue. A fairer approach would be 'contraction and convergence'. The idea here is to establish per-capita allowances on a country-by-country basis for waste emissions, harvesting of renewable resources and extraction of non-renewable resources, all of which would be managed under a total ecological 'cap'. There would be a process of 'convergence' over time between rich and poor countries. Initially developing nations would be allotted a larger share of the global budget of emissions and resources, a kind of catch-up period. Eventually, national shares would 'contract' to an equal per-capita basis proportional to population. The final contraction target would be contained within agreed environmental limits for the planet.[17]

Given the discouraging lack of progress at recent international climate talks this kind of global planning may seem like a pipedream. But there are not a lot of other options. *Sauve qui peut* isn't going to work any more in a deeply interconnected world where collective problems require co-operative solutions.

Sharing out the work

This is always a thorny issue, since employment is the siren call of growth. Productivity gains (via improved technology) translate into fewer jobs. So even with a stable population the economy must grow to create jobs for those who want to work. Even so, increased GDP is not an automatic guarantee of more jobs. Witness the slow pace of the recent 'jobless recovery' in the West.

In a zero-growth economy, with output capped

for ecological reasons, jobs would be shared and increases in productivity would be taken as more free time, helping to restore the balance between work and home. A 'steady state' may even boost jobs, since the rising prices of both energy and resources would make labor relatively cheaper and could, over time, reverse the historical trend of replacing workers with machines.

Then of course there is the public sphere, a frequent target of the Right, which derides the 'over-paid', 'coddled' state sector and the 'gold-plated' pensions of government employees. But in the transition to a zero-growth economy the government will need to backstop the job-creation process. There is much useful and necessary work to be done rebuilding essential infrastructure and patching up the social safety net that has become so frayed during the last three decades of neoliberal cuts.

Investing in public goods

The growth imperative lies at the heart of capitalist economics. Investors demand a return on their capital, which in turn spurs the drive for profit via growth. Competition fuels increased productivity (more output for each unit of investment) but eventually that leads to overproduction and, ultimately, declining rates of profit. Additional new investment is then needed to boost productivity, increase market share and profitability. Growth is not an add-on; it is woven into the market system.

A new economics of sustainability would tip the pattern of investment towards non-material production: more public goods and fewer private status goods. Ecological investment would require capital to be patient and rooted, with shorter periods of return and lower interest rates. Higher productivity would not be the goal. With a robust system of 'green taxes', investments in resource-depleting, pollution-heavy industries would be less profitable and become less attractive. A capital tax on business, based on the amount of capital deployed, would also favor investment in people over productive assets, an important shift in the transition to a zero-growth economy.

In the US recently there has been a move towards 'benefit corporations' or 'B-Corporations'. This is an attempt to redefine the responsibilities of a corporation away from a narrow focus on profit and market efficiency, a step which could theoretically help to dethrone growth as the primary metric of corporate success. At the moment a corporation is legally obliged to maximize the return on investment for shareholders. The idea of a 'benefit corporation' is that business is embedded in a network of social and cultural relationships. A B-corporation enshrines those relationships in its articles of incorporation. When deciding how to run the business, company directors must look beyond narrow financial interests. They have to consider the workers and customers as well as the suppliers, the community and the environment. The B-corporation movement is small and mostly confined to the US. But it is growing.

Putting the free-trade genie back in the bottle

In our era of economic globalization, free trade, coupled with capital mobility, means corporations have the upper hand, playing nation against nation, driving down wages internationally and externalizing environmental costs. Global trade agreements now facilitate this outmoded orthodoxy of export-led growth.

But in a global system geared to exports every country cannot come out on top. One nation's trade surplus is another's deficit. Any attempt to slow growth would mean reducing the volume of international trade, with a short-term bias towards poor countries in the Global South that need export earnings to bolster national income and fight poverty.

A no-growth economy would reduce international trade but not end it. Goods and services should be produced locally whenever possible. At the moment global free trade is powered by cheap energy from fossil fuels, cheap labor in the poorest nations and discount-priced natural resources. Environmental costs are 'externalized' – in other words, not included in the cost of production. The public picks up the bill and the planet suffers. The fast-growing 'localization' movement could help change that as citizens begin to understand the lunacy of a system which privileges 'price' and ignores 'cost'.

Building local economies can revitalize communities, making them stronger, more resilient and more neighborly. It can nourish human relationships and reduce environmental stress by minimizing energy use, shortening supply chains and encouraging durable goods meant to last. As the 'sinks' fill and the 'sources' dry up, prices will inevitably rise and the global economic system will careen from crisis to crisis. This is completely avoidable if we begin to unwind the bonds of the free-trade regime. But we must start now.

Countering consumerism

The culture of consumerism is exhausting our resources and despoiling the Earth. We cannot continue to consume ever more stuff on a finite planet. This is old news. Research shows that a ravenous desire for material goods does not translate into more happiness. Yet to keep growing the economy demands ever-increasing production *and* spiraling consumption. The two are linked in a deadly embrace. Moreover, the process of 'commodification' – turning even public services into privatized, profit-making enterprises – is rampant. The consumer ethos spreads outward from the market to infect all aspects of life.

Slowing consumer culture will require a systematic approach: thousands of commercial messages bombard us daily. Countering consumerism means creating public spaces free of consumer messages, and controlling advertising so that it provides information rather than stimulating the endless cycle of more equals better.

But it will also require a different way of 'being' in the world, where identity and meaning are forged from non-material relationships. Jumping off the treadmill of consumerism means replacing the siren call of 'more' with a more Earth-friendly acceptance of 'enough'.

I opened this guide with a reference to the barrage of criticism and disbelief that Charles Darwin faced when he introduced his theory of natural selection more than 150 years ago. The truth is that today we're captivated by a myth far more alluring than the one that constrained Darwin: the dream of perpetual growth. As a global society we have been living beyond our ecological means for decades, consuming too much and producing more waste than the environment can absorb. In the process we are eroding the future well-being of our children and grandchildren.

We've got some endgame issues facing us as a species, problems which will require us to co-operate on a global level if we are to make it through the next century without catastrophe. Climate change, resource depletion, ecological collapse and galloping consumerism: these are challenges few business or political leaders have the courage to confront. The UN itself is one checkered attempt to unite the peoples of the world in a common project of peace and prosperity. It has, to say the least, been fraught with conflict and disagreement.

We are living with an economic system that is producing vast wealth for the few at the expense of the majority. The model is broken and the damage to people, communities and the natural world is growing. In the aftermath of the great financial meltdown of

2008 and the continuing instability of the global economy, there is an urgent need – and a deep yearning – for balance and equality. The search for alternatives has never been more urgent.

1 Paul Krugman, 'The Jobless Trap', *New York Times*, 21 April 2013. **2** Richard Wilkinson and Kate Pickett, *The Spirit Level: why equality is better for everyone*, Penguin, 2010. **3** K Marx/F Engels, *The Communist Manifesto: a modern edition*, Verso, 1998. **4** Gro Harlem Brundtland, *Our common future*, Oxford University Press, 1987. **5** Ted Trainer, 'De-growth: do you realize what it means?' *Futures 44*, 2012. **6** D O'Neill/D Ben-Ami, 'Is it time to ditch the pursuit of economic growth?', *New Internationalist*, May 2013. **7** 'What Is a Steady State Economy?', steadystate.org **8** EF Schumacher, *Small is beautiful: economics as if people mattered: 25 years later ... with commentaries*, Hartley & Marks, 1999. **9** no-tar-sands.org **10** Fred Pearce, 'Greenwash: Shell betrays 'new energy future' promises', *The Guardian*, 26 Mar 2009. **11** Thomas Homer-Dixon, *The Upside of Down*, Souvenir Press, 2007. **12** Anne's name does not appear as co-author because the publisher ostensibly wanted a single author. The book is therefore listed as Paul R Ehrlich, *The Population Bomb*, Ballantine Books, 1968. **13** DW O'Neill/R Dietz/N Jones (eds), *Enough is Enough: Ideas for a sustainable economy in a world of finite resources*, Centre for the Advancement of the Steady State Economy and Economic Justice for All, 2010. **14** S Anderson/S Klinger/J Rojo, 'Corporate Tax Dodgers: 10 Companies and Their Tax Loopholes', Institute for Policy Studies, 17 Apr 2013, nin.tl/17vGVqJ **15** Marjorie Kelly, 'Can there be good corporations?', *Yes Magazine*, Spring 2012. **16** Erik Olin Wright, *Envisioning real utopias*, Verso 2010. **17** gci.org.uk

Resources

Arndt, HW, *The rise and fall of economic growth: a study in contemporary thought*, Longman Cheshire, Melbourne, 1978.

Carson, Rachel, Lois Darling and Louis Darling, *Silent Spring*, Houghton Mifflin, Boston, 1962.

Daly, Herman E, John B Cobb, and Clifford W Cobb, *For the common good: redirecting the economy toward community, the environment, and a sustainable future*, Beacon Press, Boston, 1989.

Daly, Herman E, *Steady-state economics*, 2nd ed, Earthscan, London, 1992.

Daly, Herman E, *Beyond growth: the economics of sustainable development*, Beacon Press, Boston, 1996.

Diamond, Jared M, *Collapse: how societies choose to fail or succeed*, Penguin Books, New York, 2011.

Dixon, Thomas F, *The upside of down: catastrophe, creativity, and the renewal of civilization*. Washington: Island Press, 2006.

Ehrlich, Paul R, *The population bomb*. New York: Ballantine Books, 1968.

Ewen, Stuart, *Captains of consciousness: advertising and the social roots of the consumer culture*. New York: Basic Books, 2008.

Foster, John, and Brett Clark, *The ecological rift: capitalism's war on the earth*, New York: Monthly Review Press, 2011.

Galbraith, JK, *The affluent society*, 3rd ed, Houghton Mifflin, Boston, 1976.

Gorz, Andre, *Farewell to the working class: an essay on post-industrial socialism*, South End Press, Boston, 1982.

Hansen, James E, *Storms of my grandchildren: the truth about the coming climate catastrophe and our last chance to save humanity*, Bloomsbury, New York, 2009.

Heinberg, Richard, *The end of growth: adapting to our new economic reality*, New Society Publishers, Gabriola Island, BC, 2011.

Hirsch, Fred, *Social limits to growth*, Harvard University Press, Cambridge, Mass, 1976.

Jackson, Tim, *Prosperity without growth: economics for a finite planet*, Earthscan, London, 2009.

Marchand, Roland, *Advertising the American dream: making way for modernity, 1920-1940*, University of California Press, Berkeley, 1985.

Marx, Karl, Friedrich Engels, *The Communist manifesto: a modern edition*, Verso, London, 1998.

McKibben, Bill, *Deep economy: the wealth of communities and the durable future*, Times Books, New York, 2007.

Meadows, Donella H, Jorgen Randers and Dennis L Meadows, *The limits to growth: the 30-year update*, Chelsea Green, Vermont, 2004.

OECD, *Divided we stand: why inequality keeps rising*, Paris, 2011.

Our common future, Oxford University Press, Oxford,1987.

Packard, Vance, *The hidden persuaders*, D McKay, New York, 1957.

Putnam, Robert D, *Bowling alone: the collapse and revival of American community*, Simon & Schuster, New York, 2000.

Rubin, Jeff, *The end of growth*, Random House Canada, Toronto, 2012.

Schor, Juliet, *Plenitude*, Penguin, New York, 2010.

Schumacher, EF, *Small is beautiful: economics as if people mattered: 25 years later*, Hartley & Marks, Point Roberts, Washington, 1999.

Simms, Andrew, & Victoria Johnson, *Growth isn't possible: why we need a new economic direction*, New Economics Foundation, London, 2010.

Skidelsky, Robert, *John Maynard Keynes, 1883-1946: economist, philosopher, statesman*, Penguin Books, New York, 2005.

Victor, Peter A, *Managing without growth: slower by design, not disaster.* Edward Elgar, Cheltenham, 2008.

Wilkinson, Richard and Kate Pickett, *The spirit level: why greater equality makes societies stronger*, Bloomsbury, New York, 2010.

Wright, Erik Olin, *Envisioning real utopias*, Verso, London, 2010.

World Bank, *Turn down the heat: why a 4°C warmer world must be avoided*, Washington, DC, 2012.

Organizations

Intergovernmental panel on climate change (IPPC)
ipcc.ch

The Association for the Study of Peak Oil & Gas (ASPO)
peakoil.net

Center for the Advancement of the Steady State Economy (CASSE)
steadystate.org

David Suzuki Foundation
davidsuzuki.org
earth-policy.org

Earth Policy Institute Recherche & Décroissance
degrowth.org

Global Footprint Network
footprintnetwork.org

The new economics foundation (nef)
neweconomics.org

The Pembina Institute
pembina.org

Post Carbon Institute
postcarbon.org

Sustainable Europe Research Institute (SERI)
http://seri.at/en

Transition Network
transitionnetwork.org

Worldwatch Institute
worldwatch.org

Index

Index

Index